Name _____ Date _____

Reading and Writing Numbers

Count how many crayons there are.

Example

_32_ crayons

Count how many crayons there are. Draw a line to the correct number word.

1.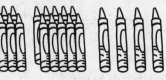

_46_ crayons

thirty-one

2.

_____ crayons

twenty-four

3.

_____ crayons

forty-six

4.

_____ crayons

thirty-seven

5. There are 3 groups of ten balloons and 6 balloons left over. How many balloons are there in all? _____

1

Use with text pages 7–9.

Ordering Numbers

Use the number line below. Complete the sentence.

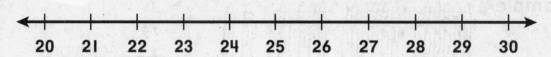

20   21   22   23   24   25   26   27   28   29   30

__20__ is just before 21.

24 is just after __23__.

Count forward.
Write the missing numbers.

Count backward.
Write the missing number.

24, __25__, __26__, 27, 28

30, __29__, 28, 27, __26__

Use the number line below. Complete the sentence.

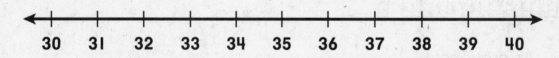

30   31   32   33   34   35   36   37   38   39   40

1. __31__ is just before 32.

2. 35 is just after _____.

3. Count forward.
   Write the missing numbers.

4. Count backward.
   Write the missing numbers.

36, _____, _____, 39, 40

35, _____, 33, 32, _____

5. Angela's sister is sixteen years old.
   How old was she two years ago?

   _____

Use with text pages 11–12.

Comparing Numbers

Count how many there are. Then compare the numbers. Are there more stars or fewer stars than boxes?

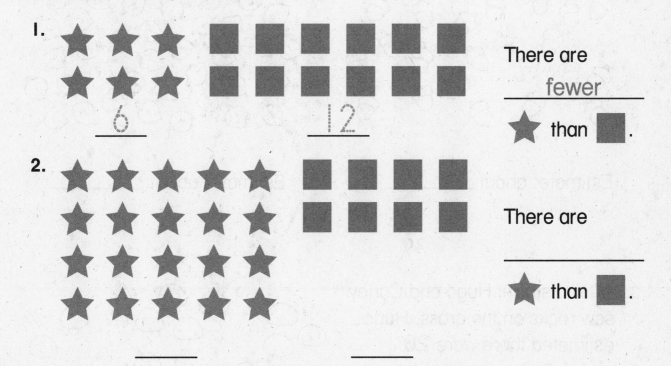

There are

_____more_____

⭐ than ⬛ .

15   8

Write how many there are.
Then write **more** or **fewer**.

1.

There are

_____fewer_____

⭐ than ⬛ .

6   12

2.

There are

_____

⭐ than ⬛ .

_____   _____

3. I am less than 45. I am greater than 43. What number am I? _____

Use with text pages 13–15.

Estimating How Many

Estimate how many. Circle a group of ten.
Use this group to help you estimate.

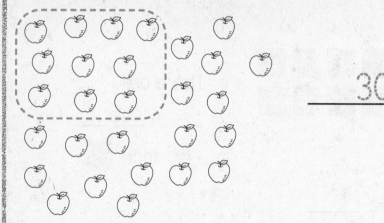

_____30_____

Estimate how many.

1.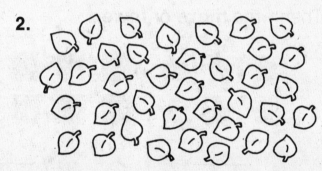

Estimate: about _____20_____

2.

Estimate: about _____

3. After a storm, Hugo and Carley saw rocks on the grass. Hugo estimated there were 20 rocks. Carley estimated there were 10 rocks. Who gave the better estimate?

_____

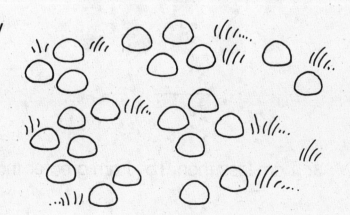

Use with text pages 17–18.

4

Name _____ Date _____

Decision: Reasonable Answers

Some answers make sense. Other answers do not.

There are 6 dogs and 4 cats in the park. Are there more dogs or more cats in the park?

10 dogs   (more dogs)   more cats

The reasonable answer is _____ more dogs _____.

Find the most reasonable answer.

Explain your answers to a family member.

1. Jill is stringing beads. What bead comes next?

    6   circle

2. There are 7 children at the lunch table. 3 children leave. How many children are left?

    7   more children   4

3. There are 3 teachers outside the school. Then 2 other teachers join them. Are there more or fewer teachers now?

    6 teachers

    more teachers

    fewer teachers

4. Jen has 5 fish. Nina has 2 turtles. How many pets do they have together?

    3 pets

    7 pets

    no pets

Use with text pages 19–20.

Name _____ Date _____

Addition Properties

Add numbers in any order The sum is the same.	Add zero to any number. The sum is that number.
$2 + 1 = \underline{3}$ $1 + 2 = \underline{3}$	$5 + 0 = \underline{5}$

Add.

1. $\begin{array}{r} 4 \\ +5 \\ \hline 9 \end{array}$ $\begin{array}{r} 5 \\ +4 \\ \hline 9 \end{array}$

2. $\begin{array}{r} 9 \\ +0 \\ \hline \end{array}$ $\begin{array}{r} 0 \\ +9 \\ \hline \end{array}$

3. $\begin{array}{r} 6 \\ +3 \\ \hline \end{array}$ $\begin{array}{r} 3 \\ +6 \\ \hline \end{array}$

4. $0 + 1 = \underline{\quad}$

    $1 + 0 = \underline{\quad}$

5. $3 + 5 = \underline{\quad}$

    $5 + 3 = \underline{\quad}$

6. $0 + 7 = \underline{\quad}$

    $7 + 0 = \underline{\quad}$

7. Frank has 3 toy cars in his left hand and 4 toy cars in his right hand. How many toy cars does he have in all?

    _____

Does it matter if you count the toys in the left hand or right hand first? Explain your answer.

_____

_____

Use with text pages 27–28.

Name _____ Date _____

Count On to Add

Use the number line. Count on to add.

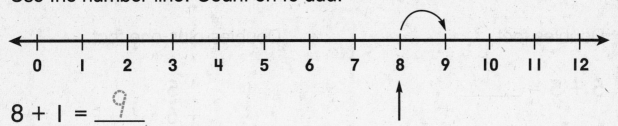

$8 + 1 = \underline{9}$

Use the number line. Count on to add.

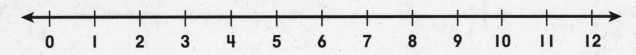

1. $5 + 2 = \underline{7}$

2. $6 + 3 = \underline{}$

3. $8 + 1 = \underline{}$

4. $3 + 4 = \underline{}$

5. $\begin{array}{r} 8 \\ + 2 \\ \hline \end{array}$

6. $\begin{array}{r} 9 \\ + 1 \\ \hline \end{array}$

7. $\begin{array}{r} 5 \\ + 2 \\ \hline \end{array}$

8. $\begin{array}{r} 7 \\ + 2 \\ \hline \end{array}$

9. 7 children and 3 adults arrive
for a party. How many people
arrive in all?

_____ people

Use with text pages 29–30.

Use Doubles Facts

Doubles facts can help you add.

Doubles fact.	Doubles-plus-one fact.

$5 + 5 = \underline{10}$

The addends are the same.

$$\begin{array}{r} 5 \\ + 6 \\ \hline 11 \end{array}$$

Think $5 + 5 + 1$.

Find the sum.

1.
$$\begin{array}{r} 2 \\ + 2 \\ \hline 4 \end{array} \qquad \begin{array}{r} 2 \\ + 3 \\ \hline 5 \end{array} \qquad \begin{array}{r} 3 \\ + 2 \\ \hline 5 \end{array}$$

2.
$$\begin{array}{r} 5 \\ + 5 \\ \hline \end{array} \qquad \begin{array}{r} 5 \\ + 6 \\ \hline \end{array} \qquad \begin{array}{r} 6 \\ + 5 \\ \hline \end{array}$$

3.
$$\begin{array}{r} 3 \\ + 3 \\ \hline \end{array} \qquad \begin{array}{r} 3 \\ + 4 \\ \hline \end{array} \qquad \begin{array}{r} 4 \\ + 3 \\ \hline \end{array}$$

4.
$$\begin{array}{r} 8 \\ + 8 \\ \hline \end{array} \qquad \begin{array}{r} 8 \\ + 9 \\ \hline \end{array} \qquad \begin{array}{r} 9 \\ + 8 \\ \hline \end{array}$$

5. Mac has 6 crayons. Ria gives him 7 crayons.
   How many crayons does Mac have in all?

   _____ crayons

Use with text pages 31–33.

Add 10

Use the Workmat with ⬭⬭⬭ .
Add.

1. $\begin{array}{r} 10 \\ +\ 5 \\ \hline 15 \end{array}$	2. $\begin{array}{r} 6 \\ +10 \\ \hline \end{array}$	3. $\begin{array}{r} 9 \\ +10 \\ \hline \end{array}$
4. $\begin{array}{r} 6 \\ +5 \\ \hline \end{array}$	5. $\begin{array}{r} 3 \\ +8 \\ \hline \end{array}$	6. $\begin{array}{r} 6 \\ +6 \\ \hline \end{array}$

Workmat

Use with text pages 35–36.

Make 10 to Add

Making a 10 can help you add 7, 8, and 9.
Find 8 + 4. Show 8. Show 4.

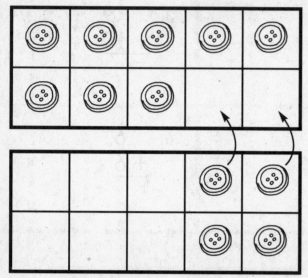

Move 2 buttons
to make 10.

How many buttons are in the top frame? __10__

How many buttons are in the bottom frame? __2__

How many buttons are there in all? __12__

Make your own Workmat. Use it with ⊙ .

Add.

1. 8 + 6 = __14__ | 2. 7 + 4 = _____ | 3. 9 + 6 = _____

4. 5
   + 8

5. 6
   + 9

6. 7
   + 7

7. Nina has 7 books about farm animals and 4 books about pets.
   How many books does she have in all? Solve by making a 10.

   _____ books

Use with text pages 37–38.

Add Three Numbers

Add three numbers. First make a 10 with two numbers.

$$\begin{array}{r} 1 \\ 4 \\ +9 \\ \end{array} \rangle 10 \qquad \begin{array}{r} 10 \\ +4 \\ \hline 14 \end{array}$$

Add three numbers. First add two numbers.

$$\begin{array}{r} 6 \\ 5 \\ +2 \\ \end{array} 11 \qquad \begin{array}{r} 11 \\ +2 \\ \hline 13 \end{array}$$

Find the sum.
Look for two numbers to add first.

1.
$$\begin{array}{r} 8 \\ 2 \\ +5 \\ \hline 15 \end{array}$$

2.
$$\begin{array}{r} 6 \\ 4 \\ +1 \\ \hline \end{array}$$

3.
$$\begin{array}{r} 5 \\ 5 \\ +3 \\ \hline \end{array}$$

4.
$$\begin{array}{r} 5 \\ 7 \\ +6 \\ \hline \end{array}$$

5.
$$\begin{array}{r} 4 \\ 9 \\ +2 \\ \hline \end{array}$$

6.
$$\begin{array}{r} 7 \\ 4 \\ +0 \\ \hline \end{array}$$

7. There are 9 birds sitting on a fence. 8 more birds
fly to the fence. 1 more bird flies to the fence.
How many birds are sitting on the fence in all?

_____

Use with text pages 39–40.

Name _____ Date _____

Problem Solving
Draw a Picture

Drawing a picture can sometimes help solve a problem.

Nina has 5 rubber balls. Sarah has 4 more rubber balls than Nina. How many rubber balls do they have in all?

Nina's rubber balls   Sarah's rubber balls

$$\underline{5} + \underline{9} = \underline{14}$$

Read. Then solve.

Draw or write to explain.

1. Inez has 9 slices of bread for sandwiches. Tony has 3 fewer slices than Inez. How many slices of bread do they have in all?

   __15__ slices of bread

2. Ali brings 6 carrots to the picnic. A rabbit eats 2 of her carrots. Donald arrives with 3 more carrots. How many carrots are there for the picnic?

   _____ carrots

Use with text pages 41–43.

Subtract All or None

Subtract zero from any number, and the difference is that number.	Subtract any number from itself, and the difference is zero.
$\begin{array}{r} 5 \\ -\ 0 \\ \hline 5 \end{array}$	$\begin{array}{r} 5 \\ -\ 5 \\ \hline 0 \end{array}$

Subtract.

1. $\begin{array}{r} 1 \\ -\ 1 \\ \hline 0 \end{array}$

2. $\begin{array}{r} 6 \\ -\ 0 \\ \hline \end{array}$

3. $\begin{array}{r} 6 \\ -\ 6 \\ \hline \end{array}$

4. $\begin{array}{r} 3 \\ -\ 3 \\ \hline \end{array}$

5. $\begin{array}{r} 9 \\ -\ 0 \\ \hline \end{array}$

6. $\begin{array}{r} 8 \\ -\ 8 \\ \hline \end{array}$

7. $\begin{array}{r} 5 \\ -\ 0 \\ \hline \end{array}$

8. $\begin{array}{r} 7 \\ -\ 7 \\ \hline \end{array}$

9. $\begin{array}{r} 8 \\ -\ 0 \\ \hline \end{array}$

10. Henry has 10 pencils. He gives all 10 pencils to his brother. How many pencils does Henry have left?

_____ pencils

11. What is the difference if you subtract all?

_____

_____

Use with text pages 51–52.

Name _____ Date _____

Count Back to Subtract

A number line can help you subtract.

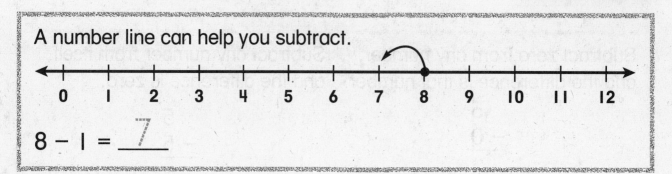

$8 - 1 =$ ___7___

Use the number line.
Count back to subtract.

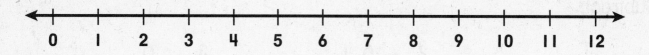

1. $7 - 3 =$ ___4___

2. $11 - 3 =$ ___

3. $8 - 3 =$ ___

4. $6 - 1 =$ ___

5. $\begin{array}{r} 10 \\ -\ 2 \\ \hline \end{array}$

6. $\begin{array}{r} 7 \\ -\ 1 \\ \hline \end{array}$

7. $\begin{array}{r} 10 \\ -\ 3 \\ \hline \end{array}$

8. $\begin{array}{r} 9 \\ -\ 3 \\ \hline \end{array}$

9. 8 children are in the park. 3 children leave.
   How many children are in the park now?

   _____ children

Use with text pages 53–54.

Subtract to Compare

Subtract to compare two sets.

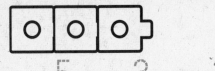

$$\underline{} - \underline{} = \underline{}$$

There are ____ fewer ▢ .

Draw circles. Draw squares.
Subtract.

1. Draw 10 circles.
   Draw 5 squares.

   | 10 | 5 |

   How many more circles
   are there?

   ____ – ____ = ____

2. Draw 7 circles.
   Draw 2 squares.

   | 7 | 2 |

   How many fewer squares
   are there?

   ____ – ____ = ____

3. Draw 11 circles.
   Draw 8 squares.

   | 11 | 8 |

   How many more circles
   are there?

   ____ – ____ = ____

Use with text pages 55–56.

Use Addition to Subtract

Addition facts can help you subtract.
They use the same three numbers.
Add or subtract.

$4 + 5 =$ _9_

$9 - 4 =$ _5_

Add or subtract.

1. $3 + 9 =$ _12_

   $12 - 3 =$ _9_

2. $5 + 6 =$ _____

   $11 - 5 =$ ____

3. $6 + 4 =$ _____

   $10 - 4 =$ ____

4. $7 + 6 =$ _____

   $13 - 7 =$ ____

5. Habib has 9 flags. He gives Pilar 3 flags.
   How many flags does Habib have left?

   _____ flags

Use with text pages 57–58.

Number Expressions

Addition and subtraction can help you name the same number.

Circle the names for 10.

(5 + 5)   10 − 5   (6 + 4)   (10 − 0)

Write names for the number.

1. | 8 | __8__ − __0__   ___ + ___   ___ − ___

2. | 7 | __4__ + __3__   ___ − ___   ___ + ___

3. | 6 | __6__ − __0__   ___ + ___   ___ − ___

4. | 12 | __6__ + __6__   ___ + ___   ___ + ___

5. | 5 | ___ − ___   ___ + ___   ___ − ___

Use with text pages 61–62.

Name _____ Date _____

Fact Families

A fact family is a set of related facts.
Fact families can help you add and subtract.

Complete the number sentences.

$6 + 7 =$ ___13___ $13 - 6 =$ ___7___

Complete the number sentences for each fact family.

1. ___6___ $+ 5 = 11$

   ___5___ $+ 6 = 11$

   $11 -$ ___6___ $= 5$

   $11 - 5 =$ ___6___

2. $3 + 4 =$ ____

   $4 +$ ____ $= 7$

   $7 -$ ____ $= 4$

   $7 - 4 =$ ____

3. $8 + 2 =$ ____

   $2 +$ ____ $= 10$

   $10 -$ ____ $= 8$

   $10 -$ ____ $= 2$

4. ____ $+ 3 = 13$

   ____ $+ 10 = 13$

   $13 - 10 =$ ____

   $13 -$ ____ $= 10$

5. Rusty tosses 2 beanbags. He gets a
   score of 12. On which 2 numbers
   could the bean bags have landed?

   ____ and ____, ____ and ____,
   or ____ and ____

4	7	9
3	5	8

Use with text pages 63–64.

Variables

Subtraction can help you find the missing numbers
in addition and subtraction sentences.

$7 + \underline{\ ?\ } = 16$

Think $16 - 7 = \underline{\ 9\ }$

The missing number is $\underline{\ 9\ }$.

Find the missing number.

1. $\boxed{} + 5 = 17$

   $17 - 5 = \underline{\ 12\ }$

2. $4 + \boxed{} = 15$

   $15 - 4 = \underline{\quad}$

3. $6 + \boxed{} = 12$

   $12 - 6 = \underline{\quad}$

4. $5 + \boxed{} = 8$

   $8 - 5 = \underline{\quad}$

5. $10 - \boxed{} = 4$

   $10 - 4 = \underline{\quad}$

6. $\boxed{} + 8 = 14$

   $14 - 8 = \underline{\quad}$

7. Marc has read 9 of his books more than once.
   He's read his other books only once.
   He has 14 books in all.
   How many books has he read only once?

   _____ books

Use with text pages 65–66.

Name _____ Date _____

Write a Number Sentence

Use a number sentence to solve a problem.

There are 6 rabbits in the garden.
5 more rabbits hop into the garden.
How many rabbits are in the garden in all?

6 + 5 = _____

Write a number sentence to solve.

Draw or write to explain.

1. There are 12 squirrels in the tree.
7 squirrels jump down. How many
squirrels are left in the tree?

____ ◯ ____ = ____

_____ squirrels

2. Chris brings 6 cans for recycling.
Rikki brings 9 cans. How many
cans did they bring in all?

____ ◯ ____ = ____

_____ cans

3. 8 birds are sitting on the fence.
4 birds fly away. How many birds
are left on the fence?

____ ◯ ____ = ____

_____ birds

Use with text pages 67–69.

Take a Survey

Wanda asked her family which fruits they liked best.

Favorite Fruits

Fruit	Tally Marks	Number
apples	I	I
bananas	III	3

Which vegetables do your family members like best?
Take a survey.

Favorite Vegetables

Vegetables	Tally Marks	Number
potatoes		
carrots		
broccoli		

Use data in your chart to answer the questions.

1. How many family members liked potatoes the best?

   _____ family members

2. Which vegetable got the most votes? _____

3. Which vegetable got the least votes? _____

4. Look at the results of the Favorite Fruits survey.
   How many family members voted in all?

   _____ family members

Use with text pages 77–79.

Name _____ Date _____

Read a Pictograph

A pictograph uses symbols to show information.

How many bananas are for sale? __6__

How many apples are for sale? __4__

Fruit for Sale

pears	▲ ▲
bananas	▲ ▲ ▲ ▲ ▲ ▲
apples	▲ ▲ ▲ ▲

Key: Each ▲ stands for 1 piece.

1. Use the table to make a pictograph. Draw 1 ◯ for every 2 balls.

Balls in Box

tennis balls	baseballs	soccer balls
||||	||||	||

Balls in Box

tennis balls	
baseballs	
soccer balls	

Key: Each ◯ stands for 2 balls.

Use the information in the pictograph to solve.

2. How many more tennis balls are there than soccer balls?

_____ rubber balls

3. If 2 baseballs get lost, how many ◯ will you take away? _____

Use with text pages 81–82.

Make and Read Bar Graphs

Jennifer asked her classmates to
choose their favorite sport.
Look at her tally chart.

Favorite Sports	
Soccer	‖‖
Baseball	‖‖
Running	‖‖‖
Swimming	‖

1. Use Jennifer's tally chart to make
   a bar graph. Color 1 box for
   each tally mark.

Favorite Sports						
Soccer						
Baseball						
Running						
Swimming						

Sports

0   1   2   3   4   5   6

Number of Children

Use the bar graph to answer the questions.

2. How many children play baseball? _____

3. Which sport did the greatest number of children choose?

   _____

4. Did more children choose baseball or running? _____

5. Which do you think is better for comparing the number of votes,
   the tally chart or the bar graph? Why?

   _____

Use with text pages 83–86.

Name _____ Date _____

Graphing on a Coordinate Grid

Use ordered pairs to find and name points on a grid.
The first number shows how many spaces right.
The second number shows how many spaces up.

Find the place on the grid.
Write the ordered pair that
names the place.

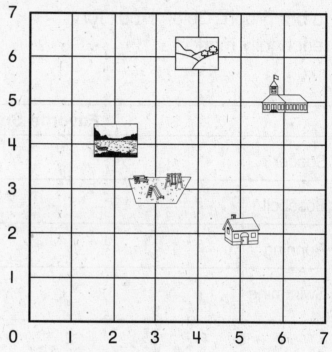

Place		Number Pair
1. house		(_5_ , _2_)
2. park		(____ , ____)
3. lake		(____ , ____)
4. hills		(____ , ____)
5. school		(____ , ____)

6. Which two places are closest to each other? Write the ordered pairs.

(____ , ____) and (____ , ____)

Use with text pages 87–88.

Range and Mode

Mode is the number that appears most often in a set of data. The range is the difference between the greatest and least numbers in a set of data.

The data shows the ages of children in after-school clubs.

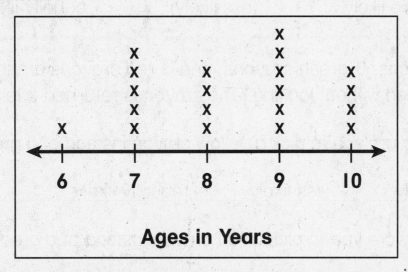

Ages in Years

Use the data to answer the questions.

1. How many children are 8 years old? _____ children

2. The fewest number of children are which age? _____ years old

3. How many children are in the clubs in all? _____ children

4. What is the mode? _____

5. What is the range? _____

Use with text pages 89–91.

Activity: More, Less, and Equally Likely

There are 5 red crayons and 5 blue crayons in a bag.
How likely are you to pick a red crayon instead of a blue crayon?
Circle.

more likely   less likely   equally likely

7 yellow crayons, 4 green crayons, and 3 red crayons are in a bag. A crayon is picked without looking. The crayon is returned after each pick.

1. How likely are you to pick a yellow crayon instead of a green crayon?

   more likely   less likely   equally likely

2. How likely are you to pick a red crayon instead of a green crayon?

   more likely   less likely   equally likely

3. How likely are you to pick a green crayon instead of a yellow crayon?

   more likely   less likely   equally likely

4. How likely are you to pick a green crayon instead of a red crayon?

   more likely   less likely   equally likely

5. Jorge also has 7 yellow crayons, 4 green crayons, and
   3 red crayons in a bag. How likely is Jorge to pick a
   green crayon or a red crayon instead of a yellow crayon?

   more likely   less likely   equally likely

Use with text pages 93–95.

Activity: Predicting Outcomes

Make a spinner that is red, yellow,
and green as shown.
What color do you think the
spinner will point to most often?

_____green_____

The largest part of the spinner is green.

1. Use a paper clip and pencil.
   Spin 10 times.
   Write your spins.

Color	Tally	Total
Green		
Yellow		
Red		

2. Which color did you land on most often?

   _____

3. Rina predicted that the spinner would
   have pointed to yellow more often
   than red? Was her prediction likely
   to happen? Explain.

   _____

Use with text pages 97–98.

Use a Graph

Data in a graph can help you solve a problem. You can use the data to add. You can use the data to compare.

You can tell that the most juices are grapefruit. You can tell that there are more orange juices than apple juices.

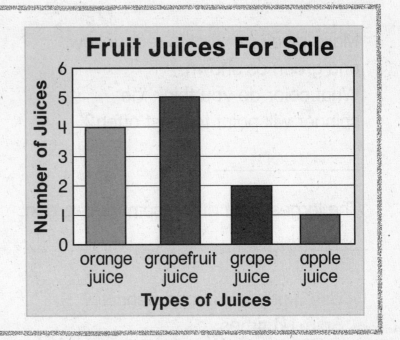

Use data in the graph to solve.

1. How many children like to go on a trip?

   _____ children

2. How many children like to play video games and read?

   _____ children

3. How many more children like to play with friends than play video games?

   _____ more

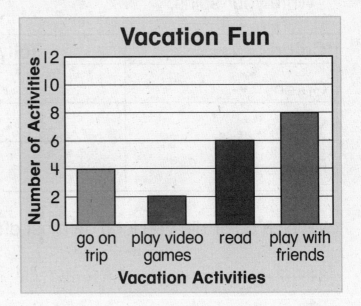

Use with text pages 99–101.

Name _____ Date _____

Tens Through 100

You can show a number using tens.
Count by tens to find the value.

  _5_ tens   _50_
                            fifty

Write the number of tens. Then write the value.

1. _4_ tens

   _40_

   forty

2. ____ tens

   ____

   eighty

3. ____ tens

   ____

   seventy

4. ____ tens

   ____

   sixty

5. Write the missing numbers.

   100, ____, 80, ____, 60, ____, 40

6. There are 10 pencils in a pack. Vinh has 3 packs of
   pencils. Raul gives him 4 more packs of pencils.
   How many pencils does Vinh have in all?

   _____ pencils

Use with text pages 123–124.

Tens and Ones to 100

7 tens 3 ones

Tens	Ones
7	3

73

seventy-three

Write the tens and ones.
Then write the number.

1. 5 tens 7 ones

Tens	Ones

_____
fifty-seven

2. 4 tens 6 ones

Tens	Ones

_____
forty-six

3. 8 tens 1 one

Tens	Ones

_____
eighty-one

4. 6 tens 0 ones

Tens	Ones

_____
sixty

5. Beverly counts the paper plates for the party.
There are 2 groups of 10 red plates.
There are 4 groups of 10 blue plates.
There are 5 white plates.

How many groups of ten plates does she
have in all?

_____ groups of ten plates

How many plates are not in a group of 10?

_____ plates

Use with text pages 125–126.

Identify Place Value

To find the value of a digit, find the value of the place it is in.

How many	Tens and Ones	Values	Number
	__6__ tens __2__ ones	__60__ + __2__	__62__

Complete the chart.

Count how many.	Write the tens and ones.	Write the values.	Write the number.
1.	_____ tens _____ ones	_____ + _____	_____
2.	_____ tens _____ ones	_____ + _____	_____

Circle the value of the underlined digit.

3. ┌─────┐
   │ 7<u>2</u> │
   └─────┘

   20   2

4. ┌─────┐
   │ <u>9</u>3 │
   └─────┘

   90   9

5. ┌─────┐
   │ 6<u>6</u> │
   └─────┘

   60   6

6. Luci has 23 flag stamps. What is the place value of the digits?

_____ tens and _____ ones

7. Biju gives Luci 9 more flag stamps. What is the place value of the digits now?

_____ tens and _____ ones

Use with text pages 127–128.

Name _____ Date _____

Different Ways to Show Numbers

You can show a number in different ways.
Circle a way to show the number.

22   (20 + 2)

Circle two ways to show each number.

| 1. | 54 | | (50 + 4) | |

| 2. | 17 | 10 + 7 | 1 ten 7 ones | 7 tens 1 one |

| 3. | 39 | | 3 tens 9 ones | 30 + 9 |

4. Richard gives Lino 2 bags of 10 apples and 3 extra apples. How many apples does Lino get? Write or draw the answer two ways.

Draw or write.

Use with text pages 131–132.

Compare Two-Digit Numbers

Use these symbols when you compare numbers:

> greater than	< less than	= equal to

20 is less than 23

20 < 23

Compare the numbers. Write >, <, or =.

1. 56 < 65
2. 76 ◯ 67
3. 20 ◯ 20

4. 29 ◯ 32
5. 95 ◯ 59
6. 55 ◯ 55

7. 60 ◯ 60
8. 21 ◯ 31
9. 48 ◯ 47

Loc has 27 marbles. Oscar has 31 marbles.
June has 4 more marbles than Loc.

Use symbols to complete the sentences.

10. The number of Loc's marbles ◯ the number of Oscar's marbles.

11. The number of June's marbles ◯ the number of Oscar's marbles.

Use with text pages 133–134.

Reasonable Answers

The most reasonable answer is the one that makes sense.

Hassan and Brianna jump rope. Hassan jumps 25 times.
Brianna jumps more than Hassan. About how many times
could she have jumped?

15 times   22 times   40 times

Circle the most reasonable answer.
Explain your answers to a family member.

1. Glen visited his cousins 10 times last year. This year he
   visits his cousins more. About how many times does he
   visit his cousins?

   6 times   10 times   14 times

2. Sue has a box of 8 crayons in her desk. Jose has a larger box of
   crayons. About how many crayons are in Jose's box?

   87 crayons   24 crayons   8 crayons

3. Oleg reads about 2 books every week. About how many
   books does he read after 6 weeks?

   4 books   15 books   50 books

Use with text pages 135–136.

Name _____ Date _____

Even and Odd Numbers

You can make groups of two to find if a number is even or odd.

| 9 | even | ⟨odd⟩ |

Draw dots. Make groups of two to show the number.
Circle **even** or **odd**.

                                                   Dots

1. | 7 | even   odd

2. | 22 | even   odd

3. | 10 | even   odd

4. | 15 | even   odd

5. | 14 | even   odd

6. There are 6 friends coming for lunch at Patti's
   house. Will she need an even or odd number of
   chairs at the table? Don't forget to include a
   chair for Patti!

_____ number of chairs

Use with text pages 143–144.

Skip Counting

Skip counting on a hundred chart shows different
number patterns.

Use the hundred chart.

1. Count by 5s.
   Color the numbers red.

1	2	3	4	5	6	7	8	9	10
11	12	13	14	15	16	17	18	19	20
21	22	23	24	25	26	27	28	29	30
31	32	33	34	35	36	37	38	39	40
41	42	43	44	45	46	47	48	49	50
51	52	53	54	55	56	57	58	59	60
61	62	63	64	65	66	67	68	69	70
71	72	73	74	75	76	77	78	79	80
81	82	83	84	85	86	87	88	89	90
91	92	93	94	95	96	97	98	99	100

Follow the pattern.
Write the missing numbers.

2. 30, 40, 50, 60, _____ , 80, _____ , 100

3. 27, 30, 33, 36, _____ , 42, _____ , 48

4. Mr. Park has 64 chickens.
   Count by 4s on the hundred
   chart. How many numbers do
   you say?

   _____

5. Mr. Park sells 8 chickens.
   Count back on the hundred
   chart to find out how many he
   has left.

   _____

Use with text pages 145–146.

Order Two-Digit Numbers to 100

You can use a number line to help you find
the position of a number.

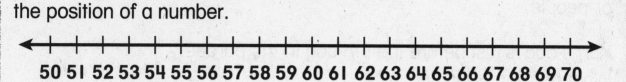

50 51 52 53 54 55 56 57 58 59 60 61 62 63 64 65 66 67 68 69 70

Find the number that comes just after.

52, __53__

Use the number line above.

Write the number that comes just after.

1. 63, __64__   2. 58, _____   3. 56, _____

Write the number that comes just before.

4. _____, 69   5. _____, 55   6. _____, 51

Write the number that comes between.

7. 60, _____, 62   8. 61, _____, 63   9. 59, _____, 61

10. The children are trying to guess
their cousin Emily's age. Myra
guessed the number just after
21. Howard guessed the
number just before 25. Emily's
age is between Myra's guess
and Howard's guess. How old
is Emily?

Draw or write to explain.

_____ years old

Use with text pages 147–148.

Name _____ Date _____

Ordinal Numbers

Ordinal numbers tell you the position of things
or people.

Karl's dog is just before the 6th dog in the parade.
What position is his dog in?

(5th)   6th   7th

Use the picture.
Circle the answer.

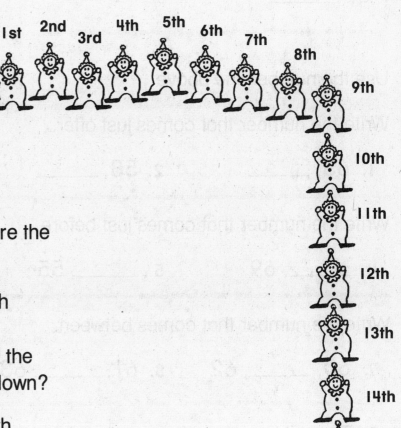

1st 2nd 3rd 4th 5th 6th 7th 8th 9th 10th 11th 12th 13th 14th 15th

1. Which clown is just
   after the tenth clown?

   9th   10th   11th

2. Which clown is just before the
   5th clown?

   fourth   fifth   seventh

3. Which clown is between the
   twelfth and fourteenth clown?

   12th   13th   15th

4. Jeni visits Mike. He used to live on the floor
   between the 13th and 15th floors. Now he
   lives 2 floors down. On what floor does
   Mike live?

   _____

Use with text pages 149–151.

Name _____ Date _____

Repeating and Growing Patterns

A repeating pattern has a pattern unit that repeats over and over again. A growing pattern gets bigger in the same way over and over again.

Continue the pattern.
First write the numbers. Then draw the next picture.

1.

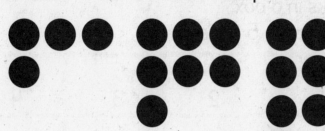

1 _____ _____ _____ _____

2.

_____ _____ _____ _____ _____ _____

3. Kristi is playing a jump-rope counting game. She says, "5, 10, 15, 20." What number comes next?

_____

Is she using a repeating pattern or a growing pattern? How do you know?

Use with text pages 153–154.

Problem Solving Find a Pattern

> Making a table can help you find a pattern.

Look for a pattern. Then solve.
Explain your answers to a family member.

1. There are 3 books in a box.
   How many books are in 5 boxes?

Number of Boxes	1	2	3	4	5
Number of Books	3	6	9	12	15

___15___ books

2. Each jar has 4 pickles.
   How many pickles are in 4 jars?

Jars	1	2	3	4
Pickles	4	8		

_____ pickles

3. Each balloon costs $2.
   How much do 6 balloons cost?

Balloons	1	2	3	4	5	6
Cost	$2	$4				

$ _____

Use with text pages 155–158.

Name _____ Date _____

Plane Shapes

 triangle circle  rectangle

 square hexagon trapezoid

Circle the shape that matches the name.

1. square

Write the name of the shape.

2.   _____

Connect the black dots to make the shape.
Write the name of the shape.

3.

_____

4.

_____

5. Ami is fitting together pieces of a puzzle. Circle the missing shape.

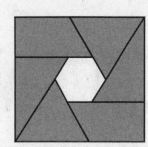

Use with text pages 179–181.

Sides and Vertices

You can describe plane shapes by the number of sides and vertices they have. A vertex is the point where two sides meet.

Write the number of sides and vertices.

 _____4_____ sides

_____4_____ vertices

 _____6_____ sides

_____6_____ vertices

Match the shapes and the sentences.

1. It has 4 vertices.

2. It has 5 sides.

3. It has 3 vertices.

4. It has 0 sides.

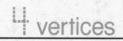

---

5. Iman drew this picture of a baseball diamond.

   What shape is it?

   _____

   How many sides and vertices does it have?

   _____ sides

   _____ vertices

Use with text pages 183–185.

Name _____ Date _____

Congruent Shapes

Shapes are congruent if they are the same size and the same shape.

Circle the shape that is congruent to the first shape.

Circle the shape that is congruent to the first shape.

1.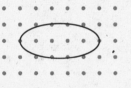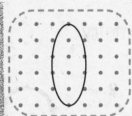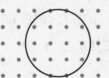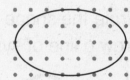

2.

3.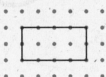

4. Look at the missing shape. Circle the shape that is congruent to the missing piece of the puzzle.

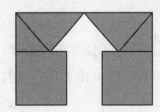

Use with text pages 187–188.

Symmetry

Shapes with a line of symmetry have equal parts.

Circle the shape that has a line of symmetry. Draw a line of symmetry.

Circle the shape that has a line of symmetry.
Draw a line of symmetry.

1.

2.

3.

4.

5.

6.

7. Matt links paper shapes for his party. Circle the shapes
   that have a line of symmetry. Draw the line.

Use with text pages 189–191.

Combine and Separate Shapes

You can take shapes apart and put them together to make new shapes.

Cut out the shapes. Make Shape A by tracing with your cut-out shapes on a sheet of paper. Then make a new shape.

Use these shapes.	Shape A	New Shape
1. 		
2.		

3. Doria made a new shape from **2** shapes. Circle the shape she made.

Use with text pages 193–194.

Slides, Flips, and Turns

You can move a shape in different ways.
You can slide, flip, or turn it.

Trace this triangle on another piece of paper.

Cut out the triangle
and put it down as shown.

1. Turn the shape.

Draw what happens.

2. Slide the shape.

3. Flip the shape.

4. Carla moved this shape. Did she
make a slide, flip, or turn?

_____

Use with text pages 195–196.

Problem Solving   Find a Pattern

Mary saw this pattern on a cup.
She drew the next three shapes in the pattern.

Draw the three shapes that come next in the pattern.

Explain your answers to a family member.

1. Marta saw this pattern on beads.

2. Herman saw this pattern on a hat.

3. Charles saw these shapes on a belt.

Use with text pages 197–199.

Name _____ Date _____

Identifying Solid Shapes

These are solid shapes.

cube

sphere

cone

square pyramid

rectangular prism

cylinder

Write the name of the solid shape in each picture.

1.

___rectangular prism___

2.

_____

3.

_____

4.

_____

5.

_____

6.

_____

7. Claude is juggling 3 balls. What shape is he using?

_____

Draw the shape.

Use with text pages 207–208.

Name _____ Date _____

Faces, Edges, and Vertices

A face is a flat surface. An edge is where 2 faces meet.
A vertex is the point where 3 or more edges meet.

Circle the shapes that match the description.

1. 0 faces, 0 edges, 0 vertices

2. 6 faces, 12 edges, 8 vertices

3. 6 faces, 12 edges, 8 vertices

4. 5 faces, 8 edges, 5 vertices

5. 2 faces, 0 edges, 0 vertices

6. 1 face, 0 edges, 1 vertex

7. Nicole wants to wear a hat with 1 face, 0 edges, and 1 vertex.

What solid shape should her hat be?   A _____

Use with text pages 209–210.

Plane Shapes on Solid Shapes

Some solid shapes have faces. You can trace around a face to make a plane shape.

_____ circle

Trace the objects pictured on a separate sheet of paper.
Write the name of the plane shape.
Remember: Some solid shapes have different shaped faces.

I.

square

2.

_____

3.

_____

4.

_____

_____

5.

_____

6. Why can't Nelly trace this
shape?

_____

_____

Use with text pages 211–212.

Classify and Compare Solid Shapes

Shapes are alike and different.
You can give reasons for comparing shapes.

Write how the pair is alike or different.
Count the faces, edges, and vertices.

	Alike	Different
1.	Both shapes roll.	A cylinder has 2 faces; a sphere has 0 faces.
2.		
3.		

4. T'yasha wants to cover a cylinder with cut-out paper. What shape or shapes should the paper be? Circle the shape.

  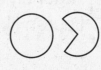

Use with text pages 215–216.

Problem Solving   Logical Thinking

Sometimes you can use clues to solve problems. The table shows the votes for each person's favorite place.

Favorite Places	
Place	**Number of Votes**
Park	12
Playground	18
Lake	7
Library	15

Nick's favorite place got more than 8 votes but fewer than 14 votes. What is Nick's favorite place? Cross out the places that do not match the clues.

___Park___   Park   ~~Playground~~   ~~Lake~~   ~~Library~~

Use the clues to find each person's favorite place.
Cross out the places that do not match the clues.
Explain your answers to a family member.

1. Simon likes the place that got more than 10 votes. It got an odd number of votes. What place does Simon like?

   ___Library___   ~~Park~~   ~~Playground~~   ~~Lake~~   Library

2. Peng's favorite place got fewer than 14 votes. It got an odd number of votes. What place does Peng like?

   _____   Park   Playground   Lake   Library

3. Lauren likes the place that got more than 14 votes. It got an even number of votes. What place does Lauren like?

   _____   Park   Playground   Lake   Library

Use with text pages 217–219.

Unit Fractions

Fractions name equal parts of a whole.
A unit fraction names one of the parts.

The fraction $\frac{1}{2}$ means 1 part of 2 equal parts.

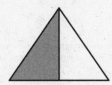 $\frac{1}{2}$

Write the fraction for the shaded part.

1.

$\frac{1}{4}$

2.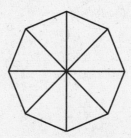

_____

3.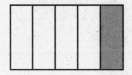

_____

4.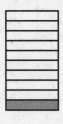

_____

5.

_____

6.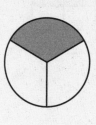

_____

7. Rory cuts a pie into 4 equal pieces. What fraction names
one part of the whole? Circle the fraction.

$\frac{1}{2}$ $\frac{1}{3}$ $\frac{1}{4}$ $\frac{1}{5}$

Use with text pages 227–228.

Name _____ Date _____

Other Fractions

Fractions can name more than one equal part of a whole.

There are 4 equal parts.
3 parts are shaded.
3 fourths are shaded.
$\frac{3}{4}$ are shaded.

Write the fraction for the shaded part.

1.

$\frac{4}{5}$

_____

2.

_____

3.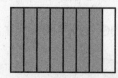

_____

4.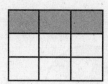

_____

5.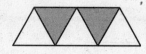

_____

6.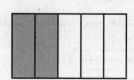

_____

7. Fold a sheet of paper in half. Fold it in half again. Turn the paper sideways and fold it again. Open the paper. Color 2 parts. What fraction did you color?

_____

Use with text pages 229–230.

54

Wholes and Parts

Fractions can name more than one whole.
Circle the fraction that names the shaded part.

$\frac{1}{2}$ $\frac{2}{2}$ $\left(\frac{3}{2}\right)$ $\frac{2}{4}$ $\frac{3}{4}$ $\left(\frac{4}{4}\right)$

Write the fraction for the shaded part.

1.

$\frac{5}{6}$

2.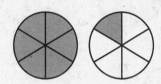

_____

3.

4.

_____

_____   _____

5. Mikki has $\frac{4}{5}$ of a sheet of paper. Does she
have more or less than a whole sheet of paper?

_____

Use with text pages 231–232.

Name _____ Date _____

Comparing Fractions

Use the symbols > to show greater
than and < to show less than
to compare fractions.

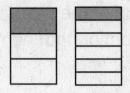

$$\frac{1}{3} \, \boxed{>} \, \frac{1}{6}$$

Compare the shaded parts. Write > or <.

1.

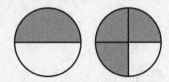

$$\frac{1}{2} \, \boxed{<} \, \frac{3}{4}$$

2.

$$\frac{4}{8} \, \bigcirc \, \frac{1}{4}$$

3.

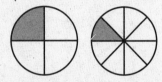

$$\frac{1}{4} \, \bigcirc \, \frac{1}{8}$$

4.

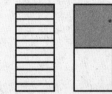

$$\frac{1}{12} \, \bigcirc \, \frac{1}{2}$$

5. You say that you can eat $\frac{1}{3}$
of a pizza. A friend says that she can
eat $\frac{1}{4}$ of a pizza. Draw two
pictures to show the two fractions.
Who can eat more? Why?

Use with text pages 235–236.

Fractions of a Set

Fractions can name parts of a set.

$\frac{2}{3}$ shaded in all $\frac{1}{3}$ not shaded

There are 3 hearts in the set. 2 of them are shaded.

$\frac{2}{3}$ of the hearts are shaded.

Write a fraction for the parts of the set.

1.

$\frac{3}{5}$ _____ shaded

$\frac{2}{5}$ _____ not shaded

2.

_____ shaded

_____ not shaded

3.

_____ shaded

_____ not shaded

4.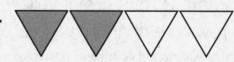

_____ shaded

_____ not shaded

5. Marcel has 10 postcards. 2 show the beach. 8 show trees. Circle the fraction of postcards that show trees.

$\frac{2}{10}$ $\frac{8}{10}$ $\frac{2}{8}$

Use with text pages 237–238.

Name _____ Date _____

Problem Solving Use a Picture

You can use a picture to find a fraction.
You can use a picture to compare two fractions.

Use the pictures to solve each problem. Color the pictures
to show fractions. Explain your answers to a family member.

1. Azim brings 10 balloons to a party.
5 of them are red. What fraction of
the balloons are red?

$$\frac{5}{10}$$

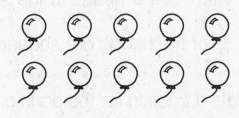

2. Sammi cuts a pizza into 8 equal parts.
She eats 2 pieces. How many pieces
of pizza are left?

_____ pieces

3. Sharon plants 5 rows of vegetables in the
garden. 2 rows are of yellow vegetables.
3 rows are of green vegetables. What
color vegetables are there more of?

_____

4. A rabbit digs up $\frac{2}{3}$ of the garden.

A puppy digs up $\frac{2}{6}$ of the garden.

Who digs up more of the garden?

_____

Use with text pages 239–241.

Mental Math: Add Tens

When you add tens, think of an addition fact.

Complete the addition sentences.
Use a basic fact to help.

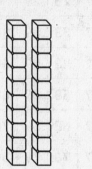 

$2 + 3 =$ __5__

$2 \text{ tens} + 3 \text{ tens} =$ __5__ tens

$20 + 30 =$ __50__

Complete the addition sentences.
Use a basic fact to help.

1. $4 \text{ tens} + 4 \text{ tens} =$ __8__ tens

   __40__ + __40__ = __80__

2. $1 \text{ ten} + 3 \text{ tens} =$ _____ tens

   _____ + _____ = _____

3. $6 \text{ tens} + 3 \text{ tens} =$ _____ tens

   _____ + _____ = _____

4. $3 \text{ tens} + 5 \text{ tens} =$ _____ tens

   _____ + _____ = _____

5. Katie has 5 sheets of stickers. There are 10 stickers on
   each sheet. Her sister Rory gives her 2 sheets more.
   How many stickers does Katie have in all?

   _____ stickers

Use with text pages 263–264.

Count On Tens to Add

Use the hundred chart. Add.

Find 44 + 30.

First find 44 on the hundred chart. Then count on by tens to add 30. Count by tens by moving down the rows.

44 + 30 = __74__

1	2	3	4	5	6	7	8	9	10
11	12	13	14	15	16	17	18	19	20
21	22	23	24	25	26	27	28	29	30
31	32	33	34	35	36	37	38	39	40
41	42	43	44	45	46	47	48	49	50
51	52	53	54	55	56	57	58	59	60
61	62	63	64	65	66	67	68	69	70
71	72	73	74	75	76	77	78	79	80
81	82	83	84	85	86	87	88	89	90
91	92	93	94	95	96	97	98	99	100

Use the hundred chart. Add.

1. 18 + 30 = __48__

2. 10 + 49 = ____

3. 40 + 17 = ____

4.   34
   + 40

5.   20
   + 13

6.   50
   + 20

7. Derek reads 17 pages in the morning. He reads 20 more pages after lunch. Then he reads 10 pages after dinner. How many pages does Derek read in all? Use the hundred chart to solve.

_____ pages

Use with text pages 265–266.

Name _____ Date _____

Regroup Ones as Tens

When you have 10 or more ones, you need to regroup.

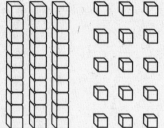

3 tens 15 ones   Regroup ⟩   __4__ tens __5__ ones | 45 |

Regroup. Write the number.

1. 3 tens 12 ones   Regroup ⟩   __4__ tens __2__ ones | 42 |

2. 6 tens 10 ones   Regroup ⟩   _____ tens _____ ones | |

3. 5 tens 17 ones   Regroup ⟩   _____ tens _____ ones | |

4. 4 tens 19 ones   Regroup ⟩   _____ tens _____ ones | |

5. Lisa has 4 sheets of stamps. There are 10 stamps in a
   sheet. She buys 16 single stamps. How many stamps
   does Lisa have in all? Regroup to solve.

   _____ stamps

Use with text pages 267–269.

Name _____ Date _____

Decide When to Regroup

If there are 10 or more ones, you need to regroup.

Solve. Use 10 attached ⊂═══⊃ to show tens.
Use single ⊂═══⊃ to show ones.

Show both numbers.	Add the ones. How many tens and ones are there?	Do you need to regroup?	What is the sum?
1. 16 + 9	__1__ ten __15__ ones	(Yes) No	25
2. 39 + 4	_____ tens _____ ones	Yes No	
3. 24 + 5	_____ tens _____ ones	Yes No	
4. 66 + 6	_____ tens _____ ones	Yes No	

5. Place 29 beans in rows of 10, 10, and 9. Then add
8 more beans. How many beans do you have in all?
Regroup to solve.

_____ beans

Use with text pages 271–272.

Add One-Digit Numbers to Two-Digit Numbers

Use these steps to add a one-digit number to a two-digit number with regrouping.

| **Step 1** Add the ones. | **Step 2** Regroup 10 ones as 1 ten. | **Step 3** Add the tens. |

Use 10 attached  to show tens.
Use single ⊂══════⊃ to show ones.
Add.

1.

Tens	Ones
	4
+ 4	4
4	8

2.

Tens	Ones
2	8
+	6

3.

Tens	Ones
	2
+ 8	9

4.

Tens	Ones
9	1
+	7

5.

Tens	Ones
	5
+ 5	8

6.

Tens	Ones
1	9
+	7

7. Lesia has 32 stickers. Diana has a few stickers. Lesia adds their stickers. She has to regroup when she adds. How many stickers does Lesia have? Circle the number.

   3   5   6   8

Use with text pages 273–274.

Name _____ Date _____

Add Two-Digit Numbers

Use these steps to add two-digit numbers with regrouping.

Step 1 Add the ones.	**Step 2** Regroup 10 ones as 1 ten.	**Step 3** Add the tens.

Use 10 attached  to show tens.
Use single ⊂══⊃ to show ones.
Add.

1.

Tens	Ones
1	9
+ 2	2

2.

Tens	Ones
7	7
+ 1	4

3.

Tens	Ones
4	4
+ 1	2

4.

Tens	Ones
2	4
+ 4	7

5.

Tens	Ones
3	9
+ 3	9

6.

Tens	Ones
	4
+ 5	6

7. Yinka made 16 points playing a video game. Her teammate
made 17 points. Yinka's team received one bonus point
for each 10 points scored. How many bonus points did
her team get?

_____ points

Use with text pages 275–277.

Problem Solving
Too Much Information

Sometimes a problem has more information than you need.

Cross out any information you do not need. Then solve.
Explain your answers to a family member.

1. There are 12 children at field day.
   Later, 11 children join them. ~~Then~~
   ~~5 parents come to watch.~~ How
   many children are at field day?

   __23__ children

2. Charles watered 16 tulips
   and 15 roses. Jill watered
   10 tulips. How many tulips
   were watered?

   _____ tulips

3. Elena washes 16 carrots and
   10 apples in the morning.
   Javier washes 24 carrots
   in the afternoon. How many
   carrots were washed?

   _____ carrots

Use with text pages 279–281.

Rewrite to Add

You can rewrite addends in vertical form.
Place the first addend on top and the
second addend on bottom.

Remember to line up the ones and tens.

$29 + 67$

Tens	Ones
1	
2	9
+ 6	7
9	6

Rewrite the addends.

Add.

1. $15 + 36$

Tens	Ones
1	
+ 3	5
	6
5	1

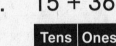

2. $9 + 47$

Tens	Ones
+	

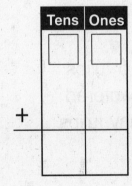

3. $73 + 14$

Tens	Ones
+	

4. $25 + 25$

Tens	Ones
+	

5. Pam rewrites $33 + 6$. She adds and gets the sum of 93.
   What did she do wrong?

   What is the correct sum? _____

Use with text pages 289–290.

Estimate Sums

When you do not need an exact sum,
you can estimate.
Estimate the sum of 22 and 37.
Round each addend to the nearest ten.
Use the number line to help you round.

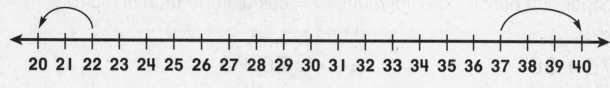

20 21 22 23 24 25 26 27 28 29 30 31 32 33 34 35 36 37 38 39 40

_20_ + _40_ = _60_

Round each addend to the nearest ten.
Estimate the sum.

10 11 12 13 14 15 16 17 18 19 20 21 22 23 24 25 26 27 28 29 30

30 31 32 33 34 35 36 37 38 39 40 41 42 43 44 45 46 47 48 49 50

1. 18 + 23

_20_ + _20_ = _40_

2. 41 + 17

____ + ____ = ____

3. 42 + 28

____ + ____ = ____

4. 50 + 35

____ + ____ = ____

5. The zoo has 28 fish and 45 birds.
About how many fish and birds does
the zoo have? Estimate to solve.

____ + __50__ = ____ fish and birds

Use with text pages 291–292.

Choose a Way to Add

Here are different ways to add: mental math,
calculator, tens and ones, and paper and pencil.
The better way to add is circled.

52 + 29	25 + 10
(paper and pencil) mental math	calculator (mental math)
75 + 38	40 + 8
(calculator) mental math	calculator (tens and ones)

Choose a way to add. Add. Explain the way you find the sum.

1. 38 + 49   Sum __87__

2. 25 + 30   Sum _____

3. 77 + 16   Sum _____

4. 30 + 7   Sum _____

5. Michelle sells 25 play tickets on Monday. She sells
   47 play tickets on Tuesday. How can Michelle find
   the total number of tickets she sells?
   How many tickets does she sell in all?

Use with text pages 293–294.

Add Three Numbers

Here are two ways to add three numbers.

Make a ten.	Use doubles.

$$
\begin{array}{r}
26 \\
34 \\
+\ 11 \\
\hline
71
\end{array}
\rangle\ 6 + 4 = 10
$$

$$
\begin{array}{r}
54 \\
14 \\
+\ 5 \\
\hline
73
\end{array}
\rangle\ 4 + 4 = 8
$$

Add.

1.
$$
\begin{array}{r}
53 \\
33 \\
+\ 2 \\
\hline
88
\end{array}
$$

2.
$$
\begin{array}{r}
44 \\
18 \\
+10 \\
\hline
\end{array}
$$

3.
$$
\begin{array}{r}
9 \\
51 \\
+26 \\
\hline
\end{array}
$$

4.
$$
\begin{array}{r}
16 \\
26 \\
+20 \\
\hline
\end{array}
$$

5.
$$
\begin{array}{r}
36 \\
11 \\
+34 \\
\hline
\end{array}
$$

6.
$$
\begin{array}{r}
13 \\
40 \\
+\ 9 \\
\hline
\end{array}
$$

7.
$$
\begin{array}{r}
11 \\
4 \\
+50 \\
\hline
\end{array}
$$

8.
$$
\begin{array}{r}
32 \\
28 \\
+\ 2 \\
\hline
\end{array}
$$

9.
$$
\begin{array}{r}
17 \\
13 \\
+25 \\
\hline
\end{array}
$$

10.
$$
\begin{array}{r}
20 \\
13 \\
+13 \\
\hline
\end{array}
$$

11. Marlene has 14 crayons. Rita has 24 crayons. Ari has 16 crayons. What two ways can you use to add the numbers?

+ _____   + _____

How many crayons do they have altogether?

_____ crayons

Use with text pages 297–298.

Problem Solving   Guess and Check

Use guess and check to solve.

    A   B   C   D

Draw or write to explain.

1. Steven buys 47 oranges.

   Which two bags does he buy?

   __A__ and __C__

---

2. The coach hands out 65
   oranges as snacks.

   Which two bags does he use
   to hand out oranges?

   _____ and _____

---

3. Manuel needs 96 oranges for
   his family party.

   Which two bags should he get?

   _____ and _____

Use with text pages 299–301.

Mental Math: Subtract Tens

When you subtract tens, think of a subtraction fact.

50 − 20

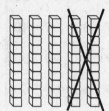

5 − 2 = __3__

5 tens − 2 tens = __3__ tens

50 − 20 = __30__

Complete the subtraction sentences.
Use a basic fact to help.

1. 8 tens − 5 tens = __3__ tens

____80__ − __50__ = __30__

2. 5 tens − 4 tens = _____ ten

_____ − _____ = _____

3. 6 tens − 4 tens = _____ tens

_____ − _____ = _____

4. 7 tens − 2 tens = _____ tens

_____ − _____ = _____

5. 7 tens − 4 tens = _____ tens

_____ − _____ = _____

6. 6 tens − 5 tens = _____ ten

_____ − _____ = _____

7. Sheets of paper come in stacks of ten. Anid has 6 stacks
of paper. She gives 3 stacks to her friend Tanesha.
How many sheets of paper does Anid have left?

_____ sheets of paper

Use with text pages 323–324.

Subtract Tens on a Hundred Chart

You can use a hundred chart to help you subtract.

76 − 30

First find 76 on the hundred chart.
Then count back by tens to subtract 30.

76 − 30 = 46

1	2	3	4	5	6	7	8	9	10
11	12	13	14	15	16	17	18	19	20
21	22	23	24	25	26	27	28	29	30
31	32	33	34	35	36	37	38	39	40
41	42	43	44	45	46	47	48	49	50
51	52	53	54	55	56	57	58	59	60
61	62	63	64	65	66	67	68	69	70
71	72	73	74	75	76	77	78	79	80
81	82	83	84	85	86	87	88	89	90
91	92	93	94	95	96	97	98	99	100

Use the hundred chart.
Subtract.

1. 38 − 20 = __18__

2. 66 − 40 = _____

3. 95 − 40 = _____

4. 26 − 10 = _____

5. 77 −20

6. 83 −50

7. 46 −10

8. 80 −70

9. Donna found 63 shells on the beach. She gave 20 shells to her sister. How many shells did Donna have left? Use the hundred chart to solve.

_____ shells

Use with text pages 325–326.

Regroup Tens

You can regroup 1 ten as 10 ones
to show a number another way.

32

3 tens 2 ones

Regroup

___2___ tens ___12___ ones

Regroup 1 ten. Use beans, buttons, macaroni, or cut-up paper.
Write the tens and ones.

1. 36   3 tens 6 ones   Regroup   ___2___ tens ___16___ ones

2. 23   2 tens 3 ones   Regroup   _____ ten _____ ones

3. 30   3 tens 0 ones   Regroup   _____ tens _____ ones

4. 27   2 tens 7 ones   Regroup   _____ ten _____ ones

5. Pens come in boxes of ten. Esther has two boxes of pens.
She wants to give away 12 pens one at a time.
She buys 2 more pens. If she only opens one box,
can she still give away 12 pens? Explain.

Use with text pages 327–328.

Decide When to Regroup

When there are not enough ones to subtract, you have to regroup.

33 – 5

3 tens 3 ones   2 tens 13 ones   2 tens 8 ones
                                                        28

Use beans, buttons, macaroni, or cut-up paper.

Show the greater first number.	Do you need to regroup to subtract?	Subtract the ones. How many tens and ones are left?	What is the difference?
1. 35 – 6	(Yes) No	__2__ tens __9__ ones	__29__
2. 49 – 8	Yes No	_____ tens _____ one	_____
3. 22 – 5	Yes No	_____ ten _____ ones	_____
4. 37 – 9	Yes No	_____ tens _____ ones	_____
5. 35 – 4	Yes No	_____ tens _____ one	_____

6. Rachel paints faces on 25 eggs. She sells 6 eggs.
   How many eggs does she have left?

   _____ eggs.

   Did she have to regroup to find the answer?
   Circle the correct answer.

   Yes   No

Use with text pages 329–330.

Name _____ Date _____

Subtract One-Digit Numbers from Two-Digit Numbers

You can regroup numbers to subtract one-digit numbers from two-digit numbers.

Subtract   44 − 6.

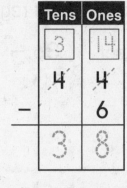

Use small items to show the numbers. Subtract.

1.

Tens	Ones
3	3
−	9
2	4

2.

Tens	Ones
2	9
−	6

3.

Tens	Ones
3	7
−	9

4.

Tens	Ones
7	3
−	2

5.

Tens	Ones
4	0
−	4

6.

Tens	Ones
2	3
−	7

7.

Tens	Ones
2	5
−	7

8.

Tens	Ones
9	8
−	8

9. Armaan has 26 balloons. On the way to the party, 7 balloons pop.

How many balloons does Armaan have left? _____ balloons.

Do you have to regroup to find the answer? Circle the correct answer.

Yes   No

Use with text pages 333–334.

Subtract Two-Digit Numbers

You can subtract two-digit numbers
with and without regrouping.

Subtract   36 − 18.

Tens	Ones
2	16
3̷	6̷
− 1	8
1	8

Use small items to show the numbers. Subtract.
Remember, sometimes you do not need to regroup.

1.

Tens	Ones
4̷	13
5̷	3̷
− 2	9
2	4

2.

Tens	Ones
6	6
− 5	6

3.

Tens	Ones
3	2
− 1	8

4.

Tens	Ones
4	1
− 3	5

5.

Tens	Ones
2	2
− 1	8

6.

Tens	Ones
5	3
− 3	4

7.

Tens	Ones
3	8
− 2	8

8.

Tens	Ones
2	4
− 1	7

9. Yolanda sells 61 plants at the fair. She sells 44 to
adults and the rest to children. How many plants
does she sell to children?

_____ plants

Do you have to regroup to find the answer?
Circle the correct answer.   Yes   No

Use with text pages 335–336.

Name _____ Date _____

Problem Solving   Use a Table

| You can use information in a table to solve a problem. |

The second grade planted trees for Earth Day.
This table shows how many trees they planted.

Trees	Number Planted
Oak trees	56
Maple trees	17
Apple trees	49
Birch trees	38

Use the table to solve each problem.
Explain your answers to a family member.

1. How many oak and maple trees
   were planted?   ___73___ oak and maple trees

2. How many more apple trees than
   maple trees were planted?   _____ more apple trees

3. How many fewer apple trees than
   oak trees were planted?   _____ fewer apple trees

4. How many maple and birch trees
   were planted?   _____ maple and birch trees

Use with text pages 337–339.

Name _____ Date _____

Rewrite to Subtract

Find 67 − 59.

You can rewrite subtraction problems
in vertical form to help you solve them.

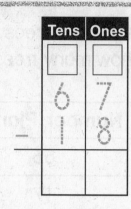 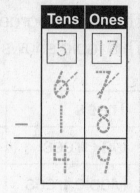

Rewrite the numbers. Subtract.

1. 41 − 19   **2.** 55 − 41   **3.** 71 − 22   **4.** 23 − 8

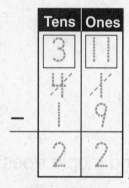 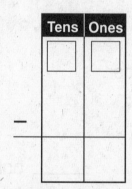 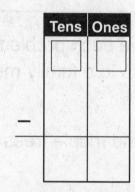 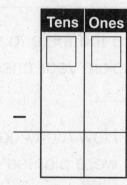

5. 78 − 22   **6.** 33 − 16   **7.** 40 − 17   **8.** 88 − 45

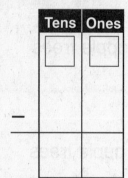 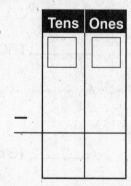 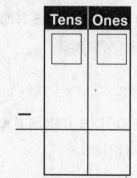

9. Gina rewrites 86 − 7 in vertical form. She subtracts and gets 16.

What did she do wrong? _____

_____

What is the correct answer? _____

Use with text pages 347–348.

Name _____ Date _____

More Two-Digit Subtraction

Subtract.

When you subtract two digits from two
digits, there are three things you must do.

36 - 19

Line up the tens and ones.
Regroup 1 ten as 10 ones and subtract.
Subtract the tens.

Tens	Ones
2	16
3	6
- 1	9
1	7

1.

5	11
6	1
- 3	5
2	6

2.

2	6
- 1	7

3.

8	2
- 3	6

4.

5	2
- 1	1

Rewrite the numbers.
Subtract.

5. 58 - 29

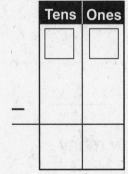

6. 50 - 6

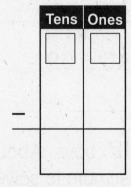

7. 75 - 35

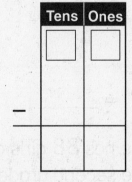

8. 88 - 19

Tens	Ones
-	

10. Mr. Duarte had 32 books. He handed out 26 books to
his students. How many books did he have left? _____ books

Use with text pages 349–350.

Estimate Differences

20 21 22 23 24 25 26 27 28 29 30 31 32 33 34 35 36 37 38 39 40

When you do not need an exact answer, you can estimate.

Round each number to the nearest ten.

Estimate the difference.

37 – 23   __40__ – __20__ = __20__

Round each number to the nearest ten.
Estimate the difference.

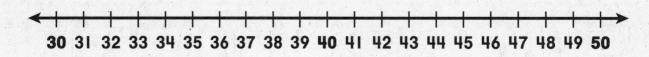

30 31 32 33 34 35 36 37 38 39 40 41 42 43 44 45 46 47 48 49 50

1. 49 – 31

__50__ – __30__ = __20__

2. 42 – 33

_____ – _____ = _____

3. 48 – 42

_____ – _____ = _____

4. 38 – 31

_____ – _____ = _____

5. 49 – 45

_____ – _____ = _____

6. 45 – 32

_____ – _____ = _____

7. 36 – 31

_____ – _____ = _____

8. 45 – 39

_____ – _____ = _____

9. The second grade has 38 girls and 45 boys. About how many children are in the second grade? Estimate to solve.

about _____ children

Use with text pages 351–352.

Choose a Way to Subtract

Here are different ways to subtract: mental math,
calculator, tens and ones, paper and pencil.

$45 - 10 = \underline{35}$

Way that I chose to subtract: mental math.

Explanation: I can count back 10 from 45 to 35.

Choose a way to subtract. Explain how you find the difference.

1. $59 - 31$

_____

_____

2. $67 - 6$

_____

_____

3. $54 - 17$

_____

_____

4. $83 - 46$

_____

_____

5. Darin had 63 crayons. He gave 27 to his friend. How can Darin find
out how many crayons he has left? _____

_____

_____

Use with text pages 355–356.

Name _____ Date _____

Use Addition to Check Subtraction

After you find the difference, you can add to check your subtraction.

$$
\begin{array}{r}
47 \\
- 28 \\
\hline
19
\end{array}
\qquad
\begin{array}{r}
19 \\
+ 28 \\
\hline
47
\end{array}
$$

Subtract.
Check by adding.

1.
$$
\begin{array}{r}
71 \\
- 4 \\
\hline
67
\end{array}
\quad + \;\square
$$

2.
$$
\begin{array}{r}
44 \\
- 14 \\
\hline
\end{array}
\quad + \;\square
$$

3.
$$
\begin{array}{r}
56 \\
- 10 \\
\hline
\end{array}
\quad + \;\square
$$

4.
$$
\begin{array}{r}
67 \\
- 18 \\
\hline
\end{array}
\quad + \;\square
$$

5.
$$
\begin{array}{r}
48 \\
- 22 \\
\hline
\end{array}
\quad + \;\square
$$

6.
$$
\begin{array}{r}
56 \\
- 9 \\
\hline
\end{array}
\quad + \;\square
$$

7.
$$
\begin{array}{r}
91 \\
- 23 \\
\hline
\end{array}
\quad + \;\square
$$

8.
$$
\begin{array}{r}
33 \\
- 19 \\
\hline
\end{array}
\quad + \;\square
$$

9.
$$
\begin{array}{r}
75 \\
- 36 \\
\hline
\end{array}
\quad + \;\square
$$

10. Alan has 39 crackers. He serves 12 crackers to his friends.

How many crackers does Alan have left? _____ crackers.

Check by adding. _____ + _____ = _____

Use with text pages 357–358.

Name _____ Date _____

Problem Solving
Choose the Operation

Decide whether you have to add or subtract to solve a problem. You can:

Add to find how many in all.
Subtract to compare two amounts.
Subtract to find one part.

Add or subtract to solve. Complete the boxes.

Draw or write
to explain

1. The second grade planted a garden. It planted
   18 bean plants. It planted 31 lettuce plants.
   How many plants did it plant in all?

   18 ⊕ 31 = 49

2. There are 22 pea plants. There are 7 potato
   plants. How many more pea plants than potato
   plants are there?

   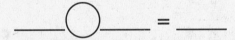

3. There are 53 tomato plants. 16 are small. The
   rest are big. How many big tomato plants are
   there?

   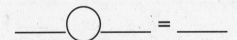

4. There are 41 pencils. There are 8 pens. How
   many more pencils than pens are there?

Use with text pages 359–361.

Pennies, Nickels, and Dimes

You can skip count and count on to find the value of the coins.
Start with the coin of the greatest value.

__10__ ¢   __20__ ¢   __25__ ¢   __26__ ¢   __27__ ¢   __27__ ¢

count on by 10   count on by 5   count on by 1   total

Find the value of the coins.

1.

__10__ ¢   __20__ ¢   ___ ¢   ___ ¢   ___ ¢   ___ ¢
                                            total

2.

___ ¢   ___ ¢   ___ ¢   ___ ¢   ___ ¢   ___ ¢
                                            total

3.

___ ¢   ___ ¢   ___ ¢   ___ ¢   ___ ¢
                                          total

4. Sergio has saved 1 dime,
2 nickels, and 4 pennies.
Count on to find the value
of Sergio's coins.

___ ¢
total

Use with text pages 383–384.

Name _____ Date _____

Quarters and Half-Dollars

A group of coins may have a half-dollar and a quarter. You can count on to find the value of the coins. Start with the coin of the greatest value.

<u>50</u>¢   <u>75</u>¢   <u>85</u>¢   <u>86</u>¢   <u>86</u>¢ total

Count on to find the value of the coins.

1.

<u>50</u>¢   <u>60</u>¢   ____¢   ____¢   ____¢ total

2.

____¢   ____¢   ____¢   ____¢   ____¢ total

3.

____¢   ____¢   ____¢   ____¢   ____¢ total

4. Debbie has 1 half-dollar, 1 quarter, 1 dime, 2 nickels, and 1 penny. Count on to find the value of Debbie's coins.

____¢ total

Use with text pages 385–386.

Name _____ Date _____

Count Coins

When you count on to find the value of coins, first put the coins in order. Start with the coin with the greatest value.

50 ¢   75 ¢   80 ¢   85 ¢   86 ¢

Use coins. Draw the coins in order.
Count on to find the value of the coins.

1.

25 ¢ 50 ¢ ____ ¢ ____ ¢

2.

____ ¢ ____ ¢ ____ ¢ ____ ¢ ____ ¢

3. Heidi has 3 pennies, 1 quarter, 1 nickel, and 2 dimes. How much money does Heidi have? Put the coins in order. Then count on to find the value.

____ ¢

Use with text pages 387–389.

Name _____ Date _____

One Dollar

100¢ has the same value as one dollar. 100¢ is written as
$1.00. You use a $ and a . to show the amount.

Write the value of the coins.
Circle the sets of coins that equal one dollar.

1.

$1.00

2.

_____

3.

_____

4.

_____

5. Konrad has 2 quarters, 1 dime, and

3 nickels. Draw the coins he has.

How much money does Konrad

have? _____

How much more money does he

need to have $1.00? _____

Draw or write to explain.

Use with text pages 391–393.

Name _____ Date _____

Equal Amounts

Different sets of coins can make equal amounts.

You can show two ways to make 75¢.

75¢   75¢

Use coins. Show two ways to make each amount.
Draw the coins.

1. 69¢

69¢

2. 87¢

87¢

3. Gina buys a book at a book sale for 86¢.
   Show two ways to make the amount.

Use with text pages 395–396.

Problem Solving
Make a List

Making a list can sometimes help
you solve a problem.

Michail wants a toy car that costs
50¢. He has quarters and nickels.
He makes a list to find the ways he
can make 50¢.

He can make 50¢ three ways.

2	
1	5
	10

Make a list to solve.

1. Maria wants a toy.
   It costs 15¢. She has
   dimes, nickels, and
   pennies.

   How many ways can
   Maria make 15¢?

   Maria can make 15¢
   _____ ways.

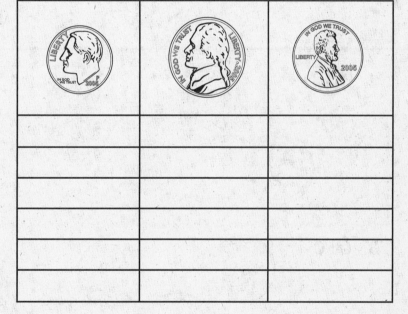

2. Jeffrey wants to buy a poster
   that costs 15¢. He has only
   nickels and pennies. Show two
   or more ways he can make 15¢.

Draw or write here.

Use with text pages 397–399.

Name _____ Date _____

Make an Exact Amount

You can use coins to show an exact amount of money.
Sometimes you choose from the coins you have.
Sometimes you need more coins.

Circle the coins that make the exact amount.

1. 75¢

2. 48¢

3. 61¢

4. Neena has all the coins shown in problem 1. She wants
   to buy a book for 92¢. So she needs more coins.
   What coins does she need?

_____

Use with text pages 407–408.

Name _____ Date _____

Compare Money Values

You can compare the values of two sets of coins.

Write the value of each set of coins. Compare.

_____55___¢ ⊖ _____55___¢

Write the value of each set of coins. Compare.

1.

_____¢ ◯ _____¢

2.

_____¢ ◯ $_____ .

3. Hector has 2 quarters and 2 dimes.
Jean has 3 quarters, 2 dimes, and 1 nickel.
Write the value of each set of coins. Compare.

Who has more money? _____ ◯ $_____ .

Use with text pages 409–410.

Name _____ Date _____

Use the Fewest Coins

You can use the fewest coins to show an amount of money.

37¢

Use the fewest coins to show the amount. Draw the coins.

1. 66¢

2. 95¢

3. 47¢

4. Helen wants to buy a plant for 83¢. Write the fewest coins she needs. _____

Use with text pages 411–412.

Name _____ Date _____

Compare Prices and Amounts

Sometimes you have to decide if you have enough
money to buy an item.

    _60_ ¢ (Yes) No

Write the amount of money.
Is there enough? Circle Yes or No.

1.     _3|_ ¢ Yes (No)

2.   ____ ¢ Yes No

3.   ____ ¢ Yes No

4. Ken wants to buy a plant. Does he have enough money?

_____

Explain. _____

Use with text pages 413–415.

Add and Subtract Amounts of Money

You add and subtract money the same way you add
and subtract two-digit numbers.

Add or subtract.		Rewrite the numbers. Then add or subtract.

$$\begin{array}{r} 64¢ \\ -\ 27¢ \\ \hline 37¢ \end{array} \qquad \begin{array}{r} 40¢ \\ +\ 40¢ \\ \hline 80¢ \end{array}$$

$84¢ - 9¢ \qquad 26¢ + 12¢$

$$\begin{array}{r} 84¢ \\ -\ 9¢ \\ \hline 75¢ \end{array} \qquad \begin{array}{r} 26¢ \\ +\ 12¢ \\ \hline 38¢ \end{array}$$

Add or subtract.

1. $\begin{array}{r} 50¢ \\ -\ 16¢ \\ \hline 34¢ \end{array}$ 2. $\begin{array}{r} 67¢ \\ +\ 24¢ \\ \hline \end{array}$ 3. $\begin{array}{r} 41¢ \\ -\ 5¢ \\ \hline \end{array}$ 4. $\begin{array}{r} 35¢ \\ +\ 11¢ \\ \hline \end{array}$ 5. $\begin{array}{r} 79¢ \\ -\ 44¢ \\ \hline \end{array}$

Rewrite the numbers. Then add or subtract.

6. $30¢ - 16¢$ 7. $78¢ + 11¢$ 8. $98¢ - 79¢$ 9. $39¢ + 5¢$

10. Reena buys a top. It costs $59¢$. She also buys a ball.
It costs $15¢$. How much money does she spend in all?

Use with text pages 417–418.

Make Change with Pennies and Nickels

When you pay more money than the price, you get change.
You can count on from the price to find the change.

Amount Paid	Price	Draw Coins to Count On			Change
25 ¢	22¢	1¢ 23 ¢	1¢ 24 ¢	1¢ 25 ¢	3 ¢

Write the amount paid. Draw the coins to find the change.

Amount Paid	Price	Draw Coins to Count On			Change
1. _____ ¢	44¢	_____ ¢	_____ ¢		_____ ¢
2. _____	85¢	_____ ¢	_____ ¢	$ _____	_____ ¢
3. _____ ¢	39¢	_____ ¢	_____ ¢	_____ ¢	_____ ¢

4. Eman bought apples for 83¢. She paid with
   4 quarters. Write the change. _____
   Draw the coins on a sheet of paper.

Use with text pages 419–420.

Name _____ Date _____

Make Change with Nickels, Dimes, and Quarters

You can make change with nickels, dimes, and quarters, too.

Amount Paid	Price	Draw Coins to Count On			Change
$1.00	55¢	10¢ 65¢	10¢ 75¢	25¢ $1.00	45¢

Write the amount paid. Count on from the price to find the change.

Amount Paid	Price	Draw Coins to Count On	Change
1. _____	20¢	_____ _____	_____
2. _____	85¢	_____	_____

3. T. J. bought a pack of pencils for 30¢. He paid
with a dollar bill. Write the change.
Draw the coins on a piece of paper. _____

Use with text pages 421–422.

Problem Solving
Act It Out with Models

Sometimes you can act out with models to solve a problem. One way is to use coins to show amounts of money.

Use coins to act out the problem.
Solve.

1. Delia has 2 quarters and 2 dimes. She wants to buy a ball for 60¢. Does she have enough money?

   _____Yes_____

2. Dani wants to buy a book for 30¢ and a plant for 45¢. She has 1 quarter and 3 dimes. How much more does she need?

   _____

3. Chris saves 1 quarter, 1 dime and 1 nickel a week. How much will he save in two weeks?

   _____

4. Nick is saving to buy flowers for his mother. He has 2 quarters, 1 dime, and 3 nickels. This is the same price as the flowers. How much are the flowers?

   _____

5. Derek has 1 quarter, 2 dimes, and 2 nickels. He wants to buy a play ticket. A ticket is 50¢. Does he have enough money?

   _____

6. Gwen has 1 quarter, 2 dimes, and 3 pennies. How much more money does she need to buy a hand puppet for 58¢?

   _____

Use with text pages 423–425.

Name _____ Date _____

Activity: Estimate Time

There are 60 seconds in one minute.
You can estimate the length of a minute.

Estimate how many times you can
do the activity in one minute.
Then do the activity for one minute.
Count the number of times you do it.

Activity	Estimate	Count
1. Count to 30.		
2. Write a friend's name.		
3. Pat your head.		

Think about the length of time.
Draw or write things you do that take that long.

4. About 30 seconds

5. About 5 minutes

6. About 1 hour

Use with text pages 433–434.

Time to the Hour and Half-Hour

There are 60 minutes in one hour.
There are 30 minutes in a half-hour.

Write the time.

__2:00__

Draw the minute hand
to show the time.

10:30

Write the time.

1.

__2:30__

2.

_____

3.

_____

Draw the minute hand to show the time.

4.

4:30

5.

3:00

6.

12:30

7. Jared watches a program about dinosaurs for a half-hour. Then he
tells Joyce about it for 30 minutes. The program started at 7:00.
What time did he finish watching and talking about the program?

_____

Use with text pages 435–436.

Time to Five Minutes

Sometimes, you can skip count by 5s to find the minutes after the hour. Start at 12.

Write the time.

5:10

Draw the minute hand to show the time.

5:40

Write the time.

1.

4:50

2.

_____

3.

_____

4.

_____

Draw the minute hand to show the time.

5.

3:25

6.

6:10

7.

9:20

8.

8:00

9. It's 1:00. Emily skip counts 5 numbers to find the minutes after the hour. This is when she has to be at the dentist. What time does she have to be at the dentist?

Use with text pages 437–439.

Name ______________________ Date ____________

Homework 16.4

Time to 15 Minutes

There are 15 minutes in a quarter-hour.

Write the time.

4:15

Draw the minute hand to show the time.

4:30

Write the time.

1. 

3:15

2. 

______

3. 

______

4. 

______

Draw the minute hand to show the time.

5. 

9:00

6. 

4:45

7. 

11:15

8. 

12:30

9. It's 3:00. Manol plays soccer 3 quarter hours from now. What time does he play soccer? ______

Use with text pages 441–442.

Elapsed Time

Counting on a clock can help you find how much time has passed.

Soccer Practice	
Start Time	End Time
3:00 P.M.	5:00 P.M.

The practice lasts

_2_ hours.

Write the times. Then write how much time has passed.

Start Time	End Time	How long does the practice last?
1. _____ A.M.	_____ P.M.	_____ hours
2. _____ P.M.	_____ P.M.	_____ hours

3. "The Sleepy Clock" starts at 7:00 P.M. and ends at 9:00 P.M.

How long is the movie? _____

Use with text pages 445–446.

Name _____   Date _____

Use a Calendar

A calendar shows the days, weeks, and months in a year. This calendar shows one month. You can use a calendar to find information.

December

Sunday	Monday	Tuesday	Wednesday	Thursday	Friday	Saturday
1	2	3	4	5	6	7
8	9	10	11	12	13	14
15	16	17	18	19	20	21
22	23	24	25	26	27	28
29	30	31				

How many days are in December? ___31___ days

How many Sundays are there in December? ___5___ Sundays

Use the calendar to answer the questions.

1. What day of the week is December 4? _____

2. What is the date of the third Monday? _____

3. How many Fridays are there? _____

4. What is the date of the second Tuesday? _____

5. On what day of the week will the next month begin? _____

6. Leza has music lessons every Thursday in December. What dates does she have music lessons?

_____

Use with text pages 447–448.

Hours, Days, Weeks, and Months

Use the words in the box. Write the best
estimate for the length of the activity.

| hours | days | weeks | months |

Playing catch

__hours__

Use the words in the box. Write the best estimate
for the length of the activity.

1. Watching a baseball game

   __hours__

2. Painting a house

   _____

3. Summer trip in a car

   _____

4. Learning a new language

   _____

5. Being in second grade

   _____

6. Practicing for a school play

   _____

7. Teaching a puppy to sit

   _____

8. Watching a play

   _____

9. Sofia visits a museum. Estimate how
   long she spends at the museum.

   _____

Use with text pages 449–450.

Problem Solving
Use a Table

Information you need to solve a problem can be in a table.

Sergio goes to three after-school activities.

How long does he spend at soccer practice?

<u>30 minutes</u>

After-School Time	After-School Activity
3:00–3:30	Soccer
4:00–5:00	Drama Club
5:00–5:30	Art Club

Solve.
Use the table and a clock to help you.

1. Bernard leaves for soccer practice at 2:30. He arrives on time. How long does it take him to get there?   _____

2. Lino paints scenery for the Drama Club. How long does Lino paint scenery?   _____

3. Angela is a member of the Drama Club. Elisa is a member of the Art Club. Who spends more time at a club?   _____

4. Amit goes to the Drama Club and Art Club. How long will he be at both clubs?   _____

Use with text pages 451–453.

Nonstandard Units

You can use ⊂══⊃ and ⊂═══ to estimate and measure length.

Object	Estimate	Measure
	about __4__ ⊂══⊃	about __5__ ⊂══⊃
	about __3__ ⊂═══	about __3__ ⊂═══

Find the real object. Use ⊂══⊃ and ⊂═══.
Estimate the length with each unit. Then measure.

Object	Estimate	Measure
1.	about __10__ ⊂══⊃	about __8__ ⊂══⊃
	about __5__ ⊂═══	about __5__ ⊂═══
2.	about ____ ⊂══⊃	about ____ ⊂══⊃
	about ____ ⊂═══	about ____ ⊂═══
3.	about ____ ⊂══⊃	about ____ ⊂══⊃
	about ____ ⊂═══	about ____ ⊂═══

4. Hugh's mom asked him to take a quick measure of the dining room table. He has a penny, a shoelace, and a toothpick. Which would you tell him to use. Why? _____

Draw or write to explain.

Use with text pages 475–478.

Name _____ Date _____

Activity: Inches

You can estimate and measure length using inches.
Length can tell how tall, how long, or how wide.

Object	Estimate	Measure
MATH	about 5 inches	about 7 inches

Find the real object. Estimate the length.
Then measure. Use an inch ruler.

Object	Estimate	Measure
1. SOAP	about _____ inches	about _____ inches
2.	about _____ inches	about _____ inches
3.	about _____ inches	about _____ inches

Compare.
Find the real object. Then measure. Circle the longest object.

4.

5.

6. Mel is on a treasure hunt. He must find something that makes noise and that is about 3 inches in length. Should he pick up a toy whistle or a toy horn?

Draw or write to explain.

Use with text pages 479–481.

Inches and Feet

An inch ruler can be used to measure inches and feet.

Object	Estimate	Measure
	about __2__ inches	about __3__ inches

Find the real object. Use inches or feet.
Estimate. Then measure.

Object	Estimate	Measure
1.	about _____ _____	about _____ _____
2.	about _____ _____	about _____ _____
3.	about _____ _____	about _____ _____
4.	about _____ _____	about _____ _____
5.	about _____ _____	about _____ _____

6. Meg needs to know if her new chair will fit though the doorway to her bedroom. The doorway is about 3 ft wide. Her chair is as wide as 2 inch rulers put together. Will her chair fit though the doorway? Explain.

Draw or write to explain.

Use with text pages 483–484.

Foot and Yard

3 feet = 1 yard   A yardstick is 3 feet.

Find	Estimate	Measure
How far apart?	about ___2 yards___	about ___3 yards___

Use feet or yards to estimate.
Then measure.

Object	Estimate	Measure
1. How far apart?	about ___3 yards___	about ___3 yards___
2. How wide?	about _____	about _____
3. How tall?	about _____	about _____
4. How wide?	about _____	about _____
5. How tall?	about _____	about _____

6. The walls in Lois's house are 10 feet tall.

The walls in Bob's house are 3 yards tall.

Whose house has the taller walls? _____.

Use with text pages 485–486.

Centimeters and Meters

You can estimate and measure length in centimeters and meters.

Object	Estimate	Measure
(spoon)	about ___12 cm___	about ___15 cm___

Find the real object.
Estimate in centimeters or meters.
Then measure.

Object	Estimate	Measure
1. (dresser)	about ___1___ ___m___	about ___2___ ___m___
2. (towel)	about ___ ___	about ___ ___
3. (rug)	about ___ ___	about ___ ___
4. (toothbrush)	about ___ ___	about ___ ___

5. Look at the four lengths. Write the lengths
   from shortest to longest.

_____ _____ _____ _____

6. Lyle has to tell the clerk in the store
   about how high he would like his new
   kitchen stool to be. Should Lyle say
   he wants a stool about 1 meter tall
   or about 10 meters tall?

Draw or write to explain.

Use with text pages 489–490.

Name _____ Date _____

Perimeter

The distance around a plane shape is its perimeter.

	$11 + 9 + 11 + 9 = 40$ The perimeter is about 40 cm.

Find the real object. Measure to the nearest meter or centimeter.
Add to find the perimeter.

1. MY LIVING ROOM FLOOR	$\underline{5} + \underline{4} + \underline{5} + \underline{4} = \underline{18}$ The perimeter is about __18__ m.
2.	_____ + _____ + _____ + _____ = _____ The perimeter is about _____ cm.
3. MY KITCHEN FLOOR	_____ + _____ + _____ + _____ = _____ The perimeter is about _____ m.
4.	_____ + _____ + _____ + _____ = _____ The perimeter is about _____ cm.

5. Nellie wants to make a pretty paper frame for her family's picture. The picture is 6 cm wide and 10 cm high. What is the perimeter of the family picture?

_____ cm

Draw or write to explain.

Use with text pages 491–492.

Name _____ Date _____

Area

You can find the area of a plane shape by using square units.

Estimate: about __15__ square units

Measure: about __18__ square units

Use square models or grid paper. Estimate.
Then find the area of the shape.

1.	Estimate: about _____ square units
	Measure: about _____ square units
2.	Estimate: about _____ square units
	Measure: about _____ square units
3.	Estimate: about _____ square units
	Measure: about _____ square units

4. Sam made a scarf. It is 15 square
   units long and 5 square units wide.
   What is the area of his scarf?

   _____ square units

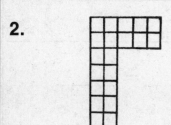

Use with text pages 493–495.

Name _____ Date _____

Use a Picture

You can use a picture to solve a problem.

| Jan wants to put an egg in each space. How many eggs does he need? ___12___ eggs | 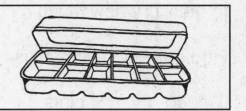 |

Solve.

1. Rikkie wants to cut carrots into strips exactly this long. How long will each carrot strip be? ___5___ cm	
2. Mrs. Dee wants to put a border on her blanket. How much ribbon does she need? _____ meters	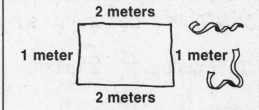
3. Dina buys two books at a fair. The books cost 37¢ and 61¢. How much does Dina pay for the books? _____ ¢	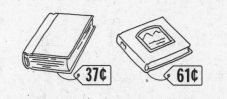
4. The coach gives out 21 oranges at soccer practice. Which two bags of oranges does he buy? bag _____ and bag _____	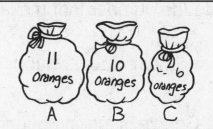

Use with text pages 497–499.

Cups, Pints, Quarts, and Gallons

You can use units such as cups, pints, quarts, and gallons
to measure how much a container can hold.

Find out which amount is greater. Circle it.

I quart   (4 pints)

Write the number that makes the sentence true.

I pint = __2__ cups

Use cup, pint, quart, and gallon measures.
Find out which amount is greater. Circle it.
Circle both if they are the same.

1. 4 cups   or   (2 quarts)   2. I gallon   or   2 quarts

3. 2 pints   or   I quart   4. I quart   or   3 pints

5. 2 pints   or   4 cups   6. I gallon   or   8 cups

Write the number that makes each sentence true.

7. 4 cups = _____ quart   8. I gallon = _____ quarts

9. Connie is making pudding. She needs 4 cups of milk.

How many pints of milk should she buy? _____

What other container of milk could she buy instead?

_____

Use with text pages 507–509.

Name _____ Date _____

Liters

You can use units such as liters and milliliters
to measure how much containers can hold.
Complete the table.

Container	Estimate	Measure
milk carton	about __1__ liter	about __1__ liter

Find the container.
Estimate how many liters it holds.
Measure.

Container	Estimate	Measure
1. 3 soup cans	about ____ liter	about ____ liter
2. juice container	about ____ liters	about ____ liters
3. bucket	about ____ liters	about ____ liters
4. big bowl	about ____ liters	about ____ liters

Circle the better estimate.

5. GLUE   20 milliliters   20 liters

6. Dave drinks 2 bottles of water. About how many liters of water does
he drink? Circle the better estimate.

   1 liter   10 liters

Use with text pages 511–512.

Pounds and Ounces

You can find objects that weigh more than a pound.

Object Name	Estimate
trash can	about __2__ pounds

Find objects that might weigh more than 1 pound.
Estimate how much you think they weigh.

Object	Estimate
1. _____	about _____ pound
2. _____	about _____ pounds
3. _____	about _____ pounds

4. Write the three objects in order
from lightest to heaviest.

_____   _____   _____

5. June is very strong. She can lift the class dictionary.
Circle about how much the dictionary weighs.

1 pound   4 pounds   16 ounces

Use with text pages 513–514.

Kilograms and Grams

You can use kilograms and grams to measure how heavy an object is.

Write **more than, less than,** or **about.**

Object	Estimate
🍌	_____ I kilogram
⬭	_____ I gram
🍎	_____ I gram

Find objects that might be more than I kilogram.
Write their names in the table.
Estimate how heavy.

Object	Estimate
I. _____	about _____ kilograms
2. _____	about _____ kilograms
3. _____	about _____ kilograms
4. _____	about _____ kilograms

Use with text pages 515–

Temperature: Fahrenheit

You can use a thermometer
to measure temperature
in degrees Fahrenheit (°F).

_____22_____ °F

Write the temperature.

1.

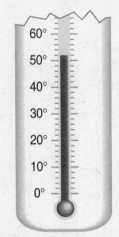

_____52_____ °F

2.

_____ °F

3.

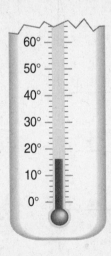

_____ °F

4.

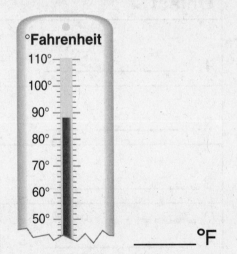

_____ °F

5. The thermometer reads 28°F. What should Felipa wear to go
outside to play? _____

Use with text pages 519–520.

Temperature: Celsius

You can use a thermometer
to measure temperature
in degrees Celsius (°C).

_____5_____°C

Write the temperature.

1.

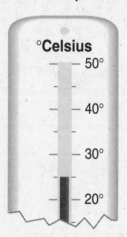

_____25_____°C

2.

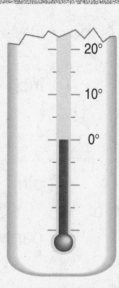

_____°C

3.

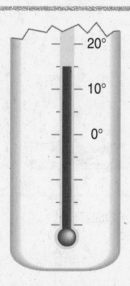

_____°C

4.

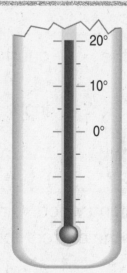

_____°C

5. The thermometer reads 35°C. Circle what Vasco can do outside.

make a snowman   swim   rake leaves

Use with text pages 521–522.

Name _____ Date _____

Measuring Units and Tools

You can use different units and different tools to measure.

How much water
is in the bowl? (cup)   pound

inch   °C

Circle the unit needed to measure. Then circle the correct tool.

1. How heavy is the   liter   pound
   football?

   inch   °C

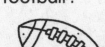

2. What is the   pint   kilogram
   temperature of
   the water?   centimeter   °F

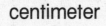

3. How tall is the   quart   pound
   table?

   inch   °C

4. Angel is cutting wood. Circle the unit needed to measure.
   Then circle the correct tool to measure.

   quart   centimeter

   pound   °F

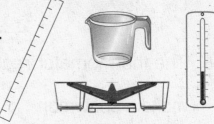

Use with text pages 523–524.

Name _____ Date _____

Reasonable Answers

When solving a problem, you should choose the most reasonable answer.

Diana's puppy is 2 feet long. The puppy grows each week. About how long is the puppy after 2 weeks?

I inch   (25 inches)   5 feet

Circle the most reasonable answer.

1. The children are playing in snow. What temperature the could it be?

   90°F   (30°F)   50°F

2. John's plant is about 7 inches tall. The plant grows each week. How tall is the plant after 3 weeks?

   6 inches   9 inches

   40 inches

3. Shira brings an apple for everyone in class. About how much does the bag of apples weigh?

   I pound   10 pounds

   100 pounds

4. Ari sells apple cider at a school fair. He arrived with 3 gallons. He sold most of the apple cider. How much does he have left?

   2 gallons   6 quarts   3 pints

5. Mica fills the fish tank. About how much water is in the tank?

   I ounce   2 pints

   5 gallons

6. About how much does Mariah's stapler weigh?

   2 ounces   I pound

   25 pounds

Use with text pages 525–526.

Name _____ Date _____

Exploring Multiplication

Make equal groups.

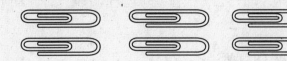

```
3 groups
2 in each group
How many in all?
```

You can add. $2 + 2 + 2 = 6$

You can skip count. 2, 4, 6

You can multiply. $3 × 2 = 6$

Use paper clips or other objects to show
equal groups. Add, skip count, or multiply
to show how many in all.

	Draw equal groups.
1. 4 groups of 2 How many in all? _____	
2. 3 groups of 4 How many in all? _____	
3. 2 groups of 5 How many in all? _____	

4. Maria puts 5 beads on a
string to make a necklace.
She makes 2 necklaces.
How many beads does she use?

Draw or write to explain.

_____ beads

Use with text pages 547–548.

Name _____ Date _____

Multiply With 2 and 5

4 groups

5 in each group

Add to find the sum.

Multiply to find the product.

$5 + 5 + 5 + 5 =$ ___20___

4 groups of 5

$4 \times 5 =$ ___20___

Find the sum.
Then find the product.

1. 3 groups of 2

$2 + 2 + 2 =$ _____

$3 \times 2 =$ _____

2. 2 groups of 5

$5 + 5 =$ _____

$2 \times 5 =$ _____

Multiply.

3. $2 \times 2 =$ _____

4. $3 \times 5 =$ _____

5. $5 \times 2 =$ _____

6. $9 \times 2 =$ _____

7. $7 \times 2 =$ _____

8. $9 \times 5 =$ _____

Circle Yes or No.

9. Sam has 2 cups. Each cup
has 5 seeds in it. He wants to
plant 12 seeds in a big pot.
Does he have enough seeds?

Yes   No

Draw or write to explain.

Use with text pages 549–550.

Multiply with 10

How many cubes are in 3 trains?

3 tens

Skip count
by 10s
10, 20, 30

$3 \times 10 =$ __30__

Write how many 10s. Multiply.

1.

_____ tens

$5 \times 10 =$ _____

2.

_____ tens

$7 \times 10 =$ _____

Fill in the number sentence.

3. Rosa has 10 plates. She
wants to put 4 strawberries
on each plate. How many
strawberries does she need?

_____ × _____ = _____

_____ strawberries

Use with text pages 551–552.

Name _____ Date _____

Multiply In Any Order

You can multiply in any order.

2 rows of 5 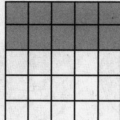 5 rows of 2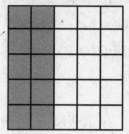

$2 \times 5 = \underline{10}$ $5 \times 2 = \underline{10}$

The product is the same.

Color to make equal rows.
Find the product.

1. 2 rows of 3   3 rows of 2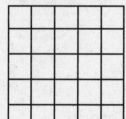

$2 \times 3 = \underline{\hspace{1cm}}$ $3 \times 2 = \underline{\hspace{1cm}}$

2. 4 rows of 5   5 rows of 4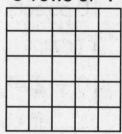

$4 \times 5 = \underline{\hspace{1cm}}$ $5 \times 4 = \underline{\hspace{1cm}}$

3. $2 \times 9 = \underline{\hspace{1cm}}$ $9 \times 2 = \underline{\hspace{1cm}}$ 4. $6 \times 5 = \underline{\hspace{1cm}}$ $5 \times 6 = \underline{\hspace{1cm}}$

5. $7 \times 2 = \underline{\hspace{1cm}}$ $2 \times 7 = \underline{\hspace{1cm}}$ 6. $6 \times 2 = \underline{\hspace{1cm}}$ $2 \times 6 = \underline{\hspace{1cm}}$

7. Jay uses cube trains to show
   that the product of 3×2 is
   the same as 2×3. Draw
   cube trains to show this.
   What is the product?

   _____

Draw or write to explain.

Use with text pages 553–554.

Share Equally

Use 12 beans or other objects and 3 bowls. Divide 12 objects into 3 equal groups.

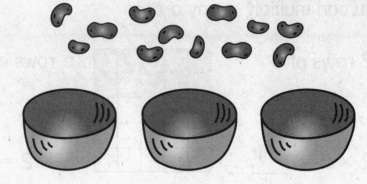

___4___ objects in each bowl

12 divided into 3 groups is 4.

$12 \div 3 =$ ___4___

Use objects and bowls.
Divide.

1. 10 objects

   2 groups

   $10 \div 2 =$ _____

   _____ in each group

2. 8 objects

   4 groups

   $8 \div 4 =$ _____

   _____ in each group

3. 12 objects

   2 groups

   $12 \div 2 =$ _____

   _____ in each group

4. 9 objects

   3 in each groups

   $9 \div 3 =$ _____

   _____ in each group

---

5. Alice, Susan, Jane and Lisa share 16 markers equally. How many markers does each friend get?

   _____ markers

Draw or write to explain.

Use with text pages 557–558.

Equal Groups of 2

How many groups of 2 can you make?

$\underline{12} \div \underline{2} = \underline{6}$

$\underline{6}$ groups

Circle groups of 2. Complete the division sentence.

1. _____ ÷ _____ = _____

   _____ groups

2. _____ ÷ _____ = _____

   _____ groups

3. _____ ÷ _____ = _____

   _____ groups

4. _____ ÷ _____ = _____

   _____ groups

5. Mark has 12 marbles.
He puts them in groups
of 2 marbles. How many
groups of 2 does he
make?

Draw or write to explain.

_____ groups

Use with text pages 559–560.

Equal Groups of 5

How many groups of 5 can you make?

__30__ ÷ __5__ = __6__   __6__ groups

Circle groups of 5. Complete the division sentence.

1.
_____ ÷ _____ = _____

_____ groups

2.
_____ ÷ _____ = _____

_____ group

3.
_____ ÷ _____ = _____

_____ groups

4.
_____ ÷ _____ = _____

_____ groups

---

5. Hannah has a roll of 20 stickers. She wants to share them equally among 5 friends. Draw a picture to show how she should divide. How many stickers will each friend get? _____ stickers

Draw or write to explain.

Use with text pages 561–562.

Problem Solving
Draw a Picture

You want to set the table for dinner.
Each person in your family needs a
fork and spoon.

How many items would you use in all?

What do you know?

1. Each person in my family needs _____ items.

2. There are _____ people in my family.

Draw a picture to solve.

3. Do you multiply or divide? _____

4. Draw a picture of each group.

5. Use the picture to help you write
   a multiplication sentence.

   _____ × _____ = _____

   _____ items

Look Back

6. How can you check your answer?

   _____

   _____

Use with text pages 563–564.

Hundreds and Tens

Count by hundreds and tens.

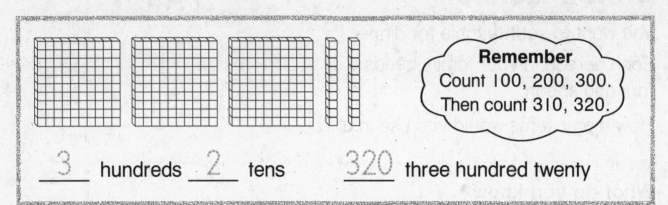

Remember
Count 100, 200, 300.
Then count 310, 320.

__3__ hundreds __2__ tens   __320__ three hundred twenty

Count by hundreds and tens. Write the number.

1.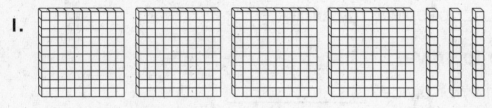

_____ hundreds _____ tens   _____ four hundred thirty

2.

_____ hundreds _____ tens   _____ six hundred forty

3.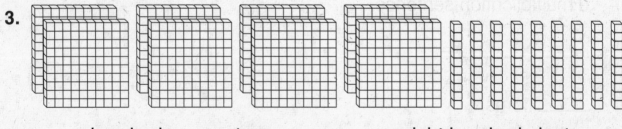

_____ hundreds _____ tens   eight hundred ninety

---

4. What number is 100 more than 760? _____

5. What number is 100 less than 600? _____

Use with text pages 573–575.

Hundreds, Tens, and Ones

Show 123.

Hundreds	Tens	Ones
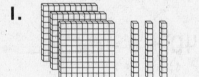		

Hundreds	Tens	Ones
1	2	3

Think
1 hundred = 100
2 tens = 20
3 ones = 3

$100 + 20 + 3 = 123$ 123 one hundred twenty-three

Count hundreds, tens, and ones.
Write how many. Write the number.

1.

Hundreds	Tens	Ones

_____

2.

Hundreds	Tens	Ones

_____

3.

Hundreds	Tens	Ones

_____

---

4. Draw hundreds, tens, and ones to show 415.

Use with text pages 577–578.

Name _____ Date _____

Identify Place Value to 1,000

Find the value of the digits in 361.

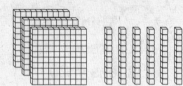

Hundreds	Tens	Ones
3	6	1

To find the value of a digit, find the value of its place.

300 + 60 + 1 _____

Write the number.

1. 400 + 20 + 5 = _____   2. 2 + 40 + 500 = _____

3. 200 + 70 + 1 = _____   4. 300 + 10 + 2 = _____

5. 6 + 30 + 100 = _____   6. 700 + 40 + 6 = _____

Circle the value of the underlined digit.

7.   52<u>8</u>

800   80   8

8.   65<u>1</u>

500   50   5

9.   <u>7</u>65

700   70   7

10.   38<u>4</u>

400   40   4

Count by 50.
Write the missing number.

11. 500   550   600   650   _____   750   _____   850

12. 250   300   350   400   450   _____   _____   600

Use with text pages 579–580.

Read and Write Numbers
Through 1,000

You can use symbols or words
to read and write numbers.

Write the number for nine hundred twenty-one. _921_

Write the word name for 345. __three hundred forty-five__

Write the number.

1. nineteen _____

2. fifty-two _____

3. one hundred thirty-seven _____

4. eight hundred twenty _____

5. two hundred sixty-seven _____

6. nine hundred twenty-five _____

Circle the word name for the number.

7. 15   fifteen   fifty

8. 214   twenty-one   two hundred fourteen

9. 940   nine hundred four   nine hundred forty

10. 624   six hundred twenty-four   six hundred twenty

11. 909   nine hundred ninety   nine hundred nine

---

12. Write a number between   _____
500 and 600 two ways.
Use numbers   _____
and words.

    _____

Use with text pages 581–582.

Name _____ Date _____

Different Ways to Show Numbers

Here are some different ways to show 314.

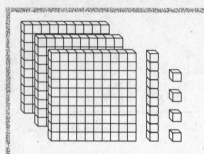   3 hundreds 1 ten 4 ones

300 + 10 + 4

Circle another way to show the number.

1. 248	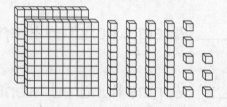	4 hundreds 2 tens 8 ones
2. 165	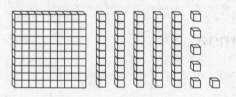	100 + 60 + 5
3. 531	500 + 10 + 3	5 hundreds 3 tens 1 one
4. 620	600 + 20	6 hundreds 2 ones

5. Amy buys stamps. She buys 1 roll of 100 stamps. She buys 3 pages with 10 stamps each. She buys 2 postcard stamps. How many stamps does she buy in all?

Draw or write to explain.

_____ stamps

Use with text pages 583–584.

Before, After, Between

Find a number before, after, or between.

640 is just **before** 641

650 is **between** 649 and 651

655 is just **after** 654

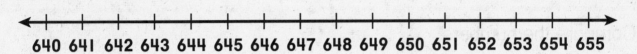

640 641 642 643 644 645 646 647 648 649 650 651 652 653 654 655

Use the number line. Write the number.

Before	Between	After
1. _649_ 650	646 _647_ 648	652 _653_
2. _____ 649	650 _____ 652	653 _____
3. _____ 653	654 _____ 656	657 _____
4. _____ 642	643 _____ 645	646 _____
5. _____ 655	640 _____ 642	651 _____
6. _____ 646	652 _____ 654	647 _____

7. Chris is reading page 115
of a book. What page is just
before 115?

Draw or write to explain.

page _____

Use with text pages 587–588.

Compare 3-Digit Numbers

Use symbols when you compare numbers.

641 is greater than 475.   339 is less than 350.

641 ⊜ 475   339 ⊜ 350

Compare the numbers.

Write >, <, or = in the ◯.

1. 525 ◯ 520	2. 212 ◯ 221	3. 144 ◯ 200
4. 763 ◯ 763	5. 838 ◯ 837	6. 626 ◯ 719
7. 1,000 ◯ 100	8. 941 ◯ 918	9. 472 ◯ 481
10. 10 ◯ 110	11. 250 ◯ 257	12. 405 ◯ 398
13. 988 ◯ 990	14. 889 ◯ 889	15. 318 ◯ 308
16. 176 ◯ 99	17. 541 ◯ 550	18. 282 ◯ 828

Circle the correct answer.

19. There are 182 apple trees. There are 128 peach trees. Are there more apple trees or peach trees?

   apple trees   peach trees

Draw or write to explain.

Use with text pages 589–590.

Name _____ Date _____

Order 3-Digit Numbers

Use place values when you order numbers.

Compare the hundreds.	Compare the tens.	Compare the ones.
3̲23 2̲20 3̲26	3 2̲ 3 3 2̲ 6	32 3̲ 32 6̲
220 is less than 323 and 326.	323 and 326 both have 2 tens.	323 is less than 326.

So, ____220____ is least.

____220____ , ____323____ , ____326____ ,

↑ least   ↑ greatest

Write the numbers in order from **least** to **greatest**.

1. 762 683 525   _____ _____ _____

2. 417 448 340   _____ _____ _____

3. 601 699 690   _____ _____ _____

Write the numbers in order from **greatest** to **least**.

4. 500 408 450   _____ _____ _____

5. 821 810 790   _____ _____ _____

6. 197 237 229   _____ _____ _____

7. Put the street numbers in order from least to greatest.

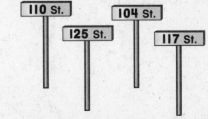

_____ _____ _____ _____ _____

Use with text pages 591–592.

Problem Solving
Make a Table

The coach orders 4 pizzas for a team party.
Each pizza has 8 slices.
How many slices are in 4 pizzas?

Solve. Make a table.
Count slices for 4 pizzas.

There are __32__ slices in 4 pizzas.

Pizzas	1	2	3	4
Slices	8	16	24	32

Make a table to solve.

1. Each pack of water has
   6 bottles. How many bottles
   are in 4 packs?

Packs	1			
Bottles	6			

_____ bottles

2. There are 10 apples in each
   bag. How many apples are
   in 3 bags?

Bags	1		
Apples	10		

_____ apples

3. Each box holds 5 pens.
   There are 20 pens in all.
   How many boxes are
   needed?

Boxes	1			
Pens	5			

_____ boxes

Use with text pages 593–596.

Mental Math: Add Hundreds

The fact $1 + 4 = 5$ can help you add $100 + 400$.

$$
\begin{array}{ll}
1 \text{ hundred} & 100 \\
+ 4 \text{ hundreds} & + 400 \\
\hline
5 \text{ hundreds} & 500
\end{array}
$$

Use the basic fact to help you add hundreds.

1. $5 + 2 =$ _____

   5 hundreds + 2 hundreds = _____ hundreds

   $500 + 200 =$ _____

2. $3 + 6 =$ _____

   3 hundreds + 6 hundreds = _____ hundreds

   $300 + 600 =$ _____

3.
$$
\begin{array}{lll}
4 & 4 \text{ hundreds} & 400 \\
+ 5 & + 5 \text{ hundreds} & + 500 \\
\hline
& \text{hundreds} &
\end{array}
$$

4.
$$
\begin{array}{lll}
2 & 2 \text{ hundreds} & 200 \\
+ 4 & + 4 \text{ hundreds} & + 400 \\
\hline
& \text{hundreds} &
\end{array}
$$

5.
$$
\begin{array}{lll}
6 & 6 \text{ hundreds} & 600 \\
+ 2 & + 2 \text{ hundreds} & + 200 \\
\hline
& \text{hundreds} &
\end{array}
$$

6.
$$
\begin{array}{lll}
3 & 3 \text{ hundreds} & 300 \\
+ 5 & + 5 \text{ hundreds} & + 500 \\
\hline
& \text{hundreds} &
\end{array}
$$

7. Trevor has 2 boxes of blocks.
   The small box has 100 blocks.
   The large box has 300 blocks.
   How many blocks are there
   in all?

   Draw or write to explain.

   _____ blocks

Use with text pages 603–604.

Regroup Ones

Show 318 and 125.

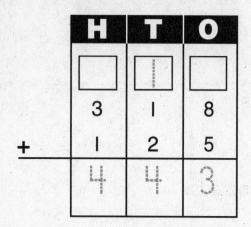

H	T	O
3	1	8
+ 1	2	5
4	4	3

First add the ones.
Regroup 10 ones as 1 ten.
Next add the tens.
Then add the hundreds.

Add.

1.   434
   + 248

2.   149
   + 323

3.   550
   + 436

4.   721
   + 159

5.   265
   + 27

6.   345
   + 202

7.   643
   +   8

8.   172
   + 114

---

9. Suki counts 65 pennies. Her brother counts 108 pennies. How many pennies do they count together?

Draw or write to explain.

_____ pennies

Use with text pages 605–606.

Regroup Tens

Find $263 + 474$.

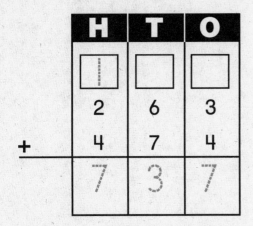

H	T	O
1		
2	6	3
4	7	4
7	3	7

> First add the ones.
> Next add the tens. Regroup
> 10 tens as 1 hundred.
> Then add the hundreds.

Add.

1. $\begin{array}{r} 152 \\ + 181 \end{array}$

2. $\begin{array}{r} 590 \\ + 238 \end{array}$

3. $\begin{array}{r} 627 \\ + 92 \end{array}$

4. $\begin{array}{r} 372 \\ + 165 \end{array}$

5. $\begin{array}{r} 486 \\ + 40 \end{array}$

6. $\begin{array}{r} 741 \\ + 198 \end{array}$

7. $\begin{array}{r} 168 \\ + 250 \end{array}$

8. $\begin{array}{r} 284 \\ + 234 \end{array}$

---

9. Lisa has 151 star stickers and 262 flag stickers. How many stickers does she have altogether?

Draw or write to explain.

_____ stickers

Use with text pages 607–609.

Name _____ Date _____

Add Money

Use a dollar sign and a decimal point
when you add money.

Find $2.25 + $0.45.

```
 $2.25
+0.45
 $2.70
```

Add.

1. $ 1.22
   + 3.18

2. $ 0.50
   + 4.50

3. $ 5.75
   + 2.51

4. $ 9.00
   + 0.08

5. $ 8.79
   + 1.05

6. $ 7.23
   + 0.90

7. $ 2.29
   + 3.52

8. $ 4.50
   + 0.66

Write the addends in vertical form.
Then add.

9. $4.01 + $0.29

10. $1.56 + $2.16

11. Kyle spends $1.49 for a pen
and $1.29 for a marker at the
school store. How much
money does he spend in all?

Draw or write to explain.

_____

Use with text pages 611–612.

Problem Solving
Guess and Check

Terrence spends $1.75 to buy 2 snacks.

Which 2 snacks does he buy?

Snacks		Supplies	
Apple	$0.50	Pencil	$0.55
Popcorn	$1.50	Notebook	$2.20
Juice	$1.25	Bookcover	$1.70

Solve. Use Guess and Check.

First Guess	**Second Guess**
$ 0.50 + 1.50 too much $ 2.00	$ 0.50 + 1.25 correct $ 1.75

Terrence buys an apple and a juice.

Use Guess and Check to solve.

1. Hannah buys 2 supplies. She spends $2.25. What does she buy?

_____ and _____

Draw or write to explain.

2. Carey buys one snack and one item from supplies. He spends $2.70. What does he buy?

_____ and _____

3. Mr. Sung spends $3.40. He buys 2 of the same item from supplies. What supplies does he buy?

_____

Use with text pages 613–615.

Mental Math: Subtract Hundreds

The fact $8 - 6 = 2$ can help you subtract $800 - 600$.

```
  8 hundreds        800
− 6 hundreds      − 600
  2 hundreds        200
```

Use the basic fact to help you subtract hundreds.

1. $5 - 3 =$ _____

   5 hundreds − 3 hundreds = _____ hundreds

   $500 - 300 =$ _____

2. $7 - 4 =$ _____

   7 hundreds − 4 hundreds = _____ hundreds

   $700 - 400 =$ _____

3.
```
   9        9 hundreds      900
 − 5      − 5 hundreds    − 500
            hundreds
```

4.
```
   6        6 hundreds      600
 − 2      − 2 hundreds    − 200
            hundreds
```

5.
```
   8        8 hundreds      800
 − 3      − 3 hundreds    − 300
            hundreds
```

6.
```
   7        7 hundreds      700
 − 1      − 1 hundred     − 100
            hundreds
```

---

7. Ms. Fox has a bag of 500 beads. She uses 100 beads to make a necklace. How many beads are left in the bag?

   Draw or write to explain.

   _____ beads

Use with text pages 623–624.

Regroup Tens

Find 362 – 148.

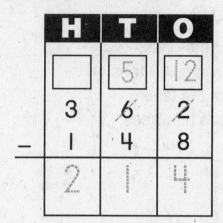

First regroup
1 ten as 10 ones.
Then subtract the ones.
Next subtract the tens.
Then subtract the hundreds.

1.

H	T	O
2	3	5
– 1	1	7

2.

H	T	O
3	8	4
–		8

3.

H	T	O
5	9	3
– 2	6	5

4.

H	T	O
4	7	1
–	4	6

5.

H	T	O
8	2	8
– 1	1	2

6.

H	T	O
7	4	6
– 2	1	9

7. It takes Earth 365 days to go
around the Sun. It takes Venus
about 225 days. How many
more days does Earth take than
Venus to go around the Sun?

Draw or write to explain.

_____ more days

Use with text pages 625–626.

Regroup Hundreds

Find 448 − 265.

H	T	O
3	14	
4	4	8
− 2	6	5
1	8	3

First subtract the ones.
Regroup 1 hundred as 10 tens.
Next subtract the tens.
Then subtract the hundreds.

Subtract.

1. 633
   − 442

2. 465
   − 182

3. 747
   − 273

4. 928
   − 397

5. 328
   − 144

6. 236
   − 151

7. 557
   − 296

8. 327
   − 45

9. 468
   − 297

10. 526
   − 293

11. 654
   − 392

12. 818
   − 626

13. Mr. Li drives 217 miles. Mr. Jones drives 135 miles. How many more miles does Mr. Li drive than Mr. Jones?

Draw or write to explain.

_____ more miles

Use with text pages 627–628.

Name _____ Date _____

Check Subtraction

Addition can be used to check subtraction.
The sum should equal the number you subtracted from.

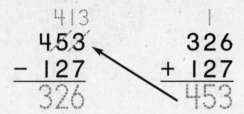

$$\begin{array}{r} \overset{4\,13}{4\,\cancel{5}\,3} \\ -\ 1\,2\,7 \\ \hline 3\,2\,6 \end{array} \qquad \begin{array}{r} \overset{1}{3\,2\,6} \\ +\ 1\,2\,7 \\ \hline 4\,5\,3 \end{array}$$

Subtract.
Check by adding.

1.
$$\begin{array}{r} 3\,6\,2 \\ -\ 1\,5\,5 \\ \hline \end{array}$$

$$+ \boxed{} \atop \boxed{} \over \boxed{}$$

2.
$$\begin{array}{r} 4\,4\,9 \\ -\ 2\,2\,8 \\ \hline \end{array}$$

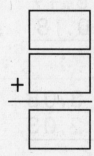

3.
$$\begin{array}{r} 5\,7\,5 \\ -\ 2\,4\,9 \\ \hline \end{array}$$

$$+ \boxed{} \atop \boxed{} \over \boxed{}$$

4.
$$\begin{array}{r} 1\,6\,6 \\ -\ \ 8\,6 \\ \hline \end{array}$$

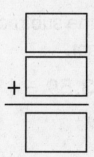

---

5. Keisha subtracts $375 - 225$
   and gets the answer 150.
   Show how she can add to
   check her subtraction.

Draw or write to explain.

Use with text pages 631–632.

Subtract Money

You use dollar signs and decimal points
when you subtract money.

Subtract $5.50 − $1.29.

$$
\begin{array}{r}
\overset{410}{\$5.\cancel{5}\cancel{0}} \\
- \;\; 1.29 \\
\hline
\$4.21
\end{array}
$$

Subtract.

1. $ 6.49
  − 0.18

2. $ 2.46
  − 1.60

3. $ 4.75
  − 1.25

4. $ 7.30
  − 4.90

5. $ 3.08
  − 2.03

6. $ 8.15
  − 3.73

7. $ 5.98
  − 2.59

8. $ 9.61
  − 5.60

Write the subtraction in vertical form.
Subtract.

9. $3.59 − $1.39

10. $5.82 − $2.25

11. Chris has $5.00. He spends
$2.50 on a drink. How much
money does he have left?

Draw or write to explain.

Use with text pages 633–634.

Name _____ Date _____

Choose the Operation

The second grade went to the Science Museum.
They spent 40 minutes at the space show.
Then they went to the exhibits for 90 minutes.

Add when you need to find how many there are in all.

How many minutes did the second grade
spend at the museum altogether?

Choose the operation.
Write + or −. Then solve.

__40__ $\left(+\right)$ __90__ = __130__ minutes

Subtract when you need to find how many more.

How many more minutes did they spend
at the exhibits than at the show?

Choose the operation.
Write + or −. Then solve.

__90__ $\left(-\right)$ __40__ = __50__ minutes

Choose the operation. Solve.

1. The bus took 65 minutes to
get to the museum and
40 minutes to return to
school. How many minutes
was the class on the bus?

Draw or write to explain.

_____ $\bigcirc$ _____ = _____

_____ minutes

2. This year 140 second graders
went on the trip. Last year
159 children took the trip.
How many more children went
on the trip last year?

_____ $\bigcirc$ _____ = _____

_____ children

Use with text pages 635–637.